THE LAW OF
SELF
DEFENSE
PRINCIPLES

By
Andrew Attorney at Law
F. Branca
Law of Self Defense LLC
www.lawofselfdefense.com

Bulk purchase discounts are available.

Send all inquiries to:
support@lawofselfdefense.com
Law of Self Defense
200 South Wilcox Street
Suite 186
Castle Rock CO 80104

Printed in the United States of America

ISBN-978-1-943809-80-6

Version: 200309

Contents

Massad Ayoob

Foreword

It may seem odd that the first guy to write books about the laws of self-defense for the legally armed private citizen would write a foreword for a competitor's book on the same topic. The reader deserves an explanation.

I wrote "In the Gravest Extreme: the Role of the Firearm in Self-Protection" in 1980. It has been a best seller ever since and remains so, not because the writer was that great, but simply because the topic is one of the most mature bodies of law in American jurisprudence. I wrote its follow-up, "Deadly Force: Understanding Your Right to Self-Defense" in 2014, with 34 more years as an expert witness in weapons/deadly force cases under my belt. Andrew's book competes directly with mine. I'm here to promote the competition?

Well, yes…simply because the competition is very, very good. Like me, Andrew makes much of his living teaching the judicious use of lethal force, and we both offer instructor classes in the subject, and teach it to trial lawyers for CLE (bar-certified Continuing Legal Education professional credit). Andrew Branca is honest, open, and above all extremely knowledgeable about his topic. He was kind enough to mention from his first book on that taking my first level class was what inspired him on this particular course. He is one of my most high-achieving graduates. I am enormously proud of him. As I wrote in "Deadly Force" and have said in multiple other venues, I think his analysis of the classic case of Florida v. George Zimmerman during the trial was the Gold Standard of such reportage. I regularly follow his commentary on other breaking cases at Andrew's blog at lawofselfdefense.com, and at legalinsurrection.com. So do most other professionals I know who go to court on these matters, and see how "the rubber meets the road."

One thing Andrew did that I didn't was to go state by state on the subtleties of case law and jury instructions. That is very important, and by itself is worth far more than the price of the book you are now about to read.

Andrew and I get a lot of each other's students, partly because we recommend each other's training to our own people, and partly because anyone smart enough to study this material before they need to put it to use train with multiple instructors … sort of like a health-conscious person "getting a second opinion."

We use different terms for some of the same principles, but any astute person can figure out that it's not about the terminology; it's about the underlying reality. If you posit the same question to two (or three, or ten, or whatever) mathematics professors, you'll get the same answer to the same problem. Confirmation is good. Double blind testing is reliable. And if those two or ten math profs each used a different formula to get to the same conclusion, the conclusion is validated all the more, and the student who understands each methodology ends up learning more.

Same here. If there is anything that Andrew and I are seen to disagree with, it's whether under the affirmative defense principle the burden of proof lies with the State. Andrew wrote, correctly, in his first and second editions of "Law of Self-Defense" and in this third edition, which I consider his best yet, that the "black letter law" says that once self-defense is raised as an issue, it is the burden of the State to prove that the defendant in a criminal case did not act in self-defense, if the prosecution hopes to win a conviction.

I've stated – in print, and in class – that I go with the definition found in "Black's Law Dictionary" that the affirmative defense shifts the burden of proof onto the defendant. When your defense is "Yeah, I shot him, but

I was right to do so," that's an affirmative defense. You are stipulating that you did the act, but maintaining that you should be held harmless for doing so.

Who is right? The great legal scholar Henry Campbell Black, or Andrew Branca, whom I consider to be a great legal scholar of modern self-defense law?

The answer is, they're both right.

The "black letter law" of the statutes quite aside, jury psychology and trial tactics are such that those of us who've lost count of our trials know that we have to show that, more likely than not, it was indeed self-defense, and "reasonable doubt" just won't cut it to win a defense verdict once your own lawyer has told the jury, "Yeah, my client killed him." In a world where altogether too many people in the jury pool can't tell "homicide" from "murder" – in a world where I've seen a lawyer scream into a TV camera "There is no such thing as justifiable homicide!" – nature tells us that yes, we will have to prove to those who judge us that more likely than not, to that greater than 50% certainty, we did indeed act in self-defense.

And if you carefully read what Andrew Branca wrote in the book you are reading now – the part where a self-defense element has to be established through testimony and/or evidence before the jury will even be allowed to hear the term "self-defense" – you'll realize that we're both speaking of the same reality of the trial courts.

You were wise to buy this book. I hope you read it, internalize it, and keep it to the forefront whenever you even think of reaching for a gun. You would be similarly wise to take Andrew's training.

Thank you for caring enough about the future of your family – who, I assure you, will go through the post-incident ordeal with you – to do so.

Massad Ayoob

About Massad Ayoob

An instructor in deadly force and firearms for police since 1972 and a full-time instructor in the field since 1982, an expert witness in weapons and homicide cases since 1979 and a certified police department prosecutor since 1988, Massad Ayoob has written twenty books on this and related topics and thousands of articles. He served two years as co-vice chair of the Forensic

Evidence Committee of the National Association of Criminal Defense Lawyers, nineteen years as chair of the Firearms/Deadly Force Training Committee of the American Society of Law Enforcement Trainers, thirteen years on the Advisory Board of the International Law Enforcement Educators and Trainers Association, and several years on the Advisory Board of the Armed Citizens Legal Defense Network and on the Board of Trustees of the Second Amendment Foundation.

Introduction

Suddenly that fearful moment you prayed would never happen has arrived.

There's a threat to your life.

It could be in any of a hundred different forms. Some are starkly unmistakable: the muzzle of a gun, a knife directing you into an alley, your front door smashing open.

Others are more ambiguous: the odd stranger stopping you to "ask for the time," a man following a little too close in a parking lot, a group of young people taking an excessive interest in you.

In whatever form the threat presents itself, your mind responds the same way: DANGER!!!! In an instant, your body floods with adrenaline, the sensation unmistakable. You last felt it when that neighborhood kid ran out in front of your car, and you braked just in time. Your body is preparing itself for an event that's not supposed to happen in a civilized society: violence.

The next few moments will be a turning point in your life. Minutes from now you might be dead, raped, maimed ... or alive, unhurt, and safe. Months from now you might be facing years in prison ... or enjoying the freedom that comes with exoneration.

The good news is that to a large extent you decide the outcome. While the physical and legal risks of violence can never be zero, you can substantially decrease those risks with the right preparation.

Some people think that the danger of violence is rare, perhaps one-in-a-million. They wonder why anyone would bother preparing for such an unlikelihood.

But consider this: There were 5.4 million murders, rapes, robberies, assaults, and sexual assaults in the US in 2014. There were another 10.9 million burglaries and thefts. That's a crime for every 20 people and a violent crime for every 60 people—in one year alone.

That's a far cry from one-in-a-million. Given the average classroom size, that's about one person in every classroom you spent time in during high school. Every single year.

This is why it's so important to be prepared. Being prepared to defend yourself against criminal predation lies at the core of what it means to be free. Protecting our future and that of our family against evil people is a fundamental human right—indeed, I would argue that it's a fundamental human duty. If you are anything like me, the alternative—to live at the mercy of evil—is simply unacceptable. I will not.

And no one is better positioned than you to take responsibility for your personal protection, and that of your family.

We've all heard the phrase, "When seconds count, the police are only minutes away." This is not a knock against the police. Many officers are good friends of mine, and no police force can be everywhere—nor, in a free country, would we want them to be.

But calling the police almost never helps in the moment of crisis. Criminals, like predators in nature, do not attack when conditions favor the prey, when the sheepdog is alert beside the sheep. Predators attack when the prey is vulnerable and unprotected. In other words, when the cops can't respond fast enough.

When an attack comes, you probably won't be standing in front of the police station. You'll be alone, or multitasking a busy life, or burdened (tactically speaking) with small children. You could even be sound asleep. Your attacker will choose that moment precisely because he thinks he can get away with it.

The mere thought of this is frightening. And that's a good thing. Properly applied, a little bit of fear keeps us alert. It is OK for children to live without fear. Indeed, that is a top priority of every parent. But adults must see the world for what it is, both very good and very bad, and prepare for the worst so they can safely enjoy the best.

The good news is that because we know how evil people target their prey, we can use this knowledge against them. Avoid looking weak, and the bad guy will seek easier prey. Stay alert and aware of your surroundings. Project confidence. Avoid places where you can get cornered, and make yourself look like more work than you're worth. Criminals are sometimes too stupid to know better, but that's the exception. If you look like difficult prey, they may well move on to someone who looks less troublesome.

Of course, sometimes nothing works. The predator decides that you're the special of the day, and you can't prevent his attack. Fortunately, most Americans today are able, if they wish, to carry a weapon that will stop the most vicious predators, even if the predator's target is comparatively small, weak, or disabled. I speak of the modern handgun, aptly identified by Samuel Colt as "the Great Equalizer."

Handguns are relatively inexpensive, common, easy to conceal, and increasingly accessible at moments of crisis, thanks to widespread improvements in concealed carry laws. Now law-abiding adults never have to be vulnerable. Should a bad guy pick them as a target, the armed person can meet the attack with fangs of his (or her) own.[1]

But winning the physical contest is far from the end of the matter. Not hardly. Because now begins the legal battle.

It's surprising, shocking even, just how much power self-defense laws grant us. Before the government can execute even the most heinous murderer imaginable, that killer must have his Miranda rights read to him, receive free legal counsel, be tried before a jury, be found guilty beyond a reasonable doubt, receive an appeal, another appeal, yet another appeal, and so on. It

---

[1] I should note that this book analyzes the law as it relates to self-defense. That doesn't mean that the defensive force must always be a gun. It could be a knife, pepper spray, or even bare hands. I strongly encourage the use of each type of defense in its proper place—not every problem is a nail, not every solution is a hammer—and I will discuss this in further detail throughout the book.

takes years to overcome the hurdles before our system approves violent action against the worst in our society.

Yet you can accomplish the same end, lawfully, with a single, small movement of your trigger finger. In an instant's decision, you can take the life of another human being, with no need for prior authorization or due process of law. So long as you can show that what you did was justified self-defense, you can walk away, free of criminal sanction.

But there's the rub. All that freedom to pull the trigger built into the front end of our system is balanced by a massive and unforgiving reckoning at the back end. Beginning before the smoke has even cleared, the justice system kicks into gear like a massive steam-era machine, with monstrous gears and pistons, to evaluate your actions under a microscope and crush you for a misstep.

This criminal justice system views self-defense like a simple light switch: either on or off. Either your actions fall within the law, and you have zero criminal liability . . . or it falls outside the law, and you have total criminal liability. There is no middle ground.

If you pass the criminal justice "machine's" examination, you go free. If not . . . well, you're probably going to miss some time at work. Maybe your kid's wedding. Maybe everything. Welcome to the end of your life as you know it. Best, then, to stay well within the lawful boundaries. But what are those boundaries? How do you get the support you need to ensure your legal "survival"? Where can you go to get help both before and after a self-defense encounter?

The first step is knowledge, and you've come to the right place.

I am sure many of you have heard stories where people defend themselves and have few difficulties afterward, legal or otherwise. There was that old lady who shot the late-night intruder or the young woman who killed the rapist dragging her from her car.

Such cases might lead you to think, "What do I have to worry about? As far as I can tell, when good people use guns for protection, they're not even arrested. Isn't a good shoot a good shoot? I'm fine."

When good people use guns to defend themselves in the right way and face no legal consequences, no one is happier than I. In truth, though, many of these people avoided a grueling legal fate because someone chose not to prosecute, not because they couldn't have done so.

Indeed, in many such cases a trained eye can see where their actions were not lawful self-defense at all. Fortunately for these well -ntentioned but mistaken defenders, the authorities didn't choose to prosecute.

But authorities will usually bring serious charges against the well-intentioned but legally mistaken "defender." Our office gets calls from folks like this all the time. Without exception they are genuinely shocked that they are in trouble. I can practically predict the call. At some point they'll say, "I can't believe I was arrested for self-defense!"

One could, of course, go through life willfully ignorant of the law and hope for the best. After all, you're one of the good guys, right? Surely they'll know that.

And you might, indeed, get lucky. But you are putting your future in other people's hands. None of the people who will be in control of your fate will understand what it was like at that desperate moment. Adrenaline was surging through your bloodstream. Your hands were cold and clammy. Your vision was tunneling. Your hearing was shutting down, and you terrifyingly realized that these might be your last moments. In contrast, those judging you will enjoy the perfect safety of a prosecutor's office or a courtroom with armed bailiffs at each door.

As far as the police and prosecutors are concerned, you're just another mug shot and case file, not all that different from the rapist they arrested yesterday or the burglar they'll get tomorrow. Both of whom, by the way, will proclaim their innocence just as loudly as you.

Given that you've always thought of yourself as one of the "good guys," it can come as a shock to find yourself disarmed, handcuffed, and dumped in the back of a cruiser. Your new title is now "Suspect." Congratulations. That guy you stopped when he tried to take your life? In the eyes of the law, he's the "Victim."

The officers responding to the scene are not there to be your friend and provide solace after a harrowing experience. They are there to determine if what happened was a crime, and find the bad guy. Unless you live in a very small town, or are prone to get into routine trouble with the law, these officers will be strangers to you. To them, you're just another face among the often unpleasant, and sometimes murderous, people they are obliged to deal with every day.

In many jurisdictions, just firing a shot automatically wins you handcuffs and a free ride to the police station for booking. This doesn't make the police good guys or bad. They're just people doing their jobs.

The people tasked with prosecuting you also don't know you. Your file is just one of many hundreds that come across their desk. They will not consider what is in your best interest. They will prosecute you if they think your case is vulnerable. Period. That's their job.

The judge knows nothing of you personally, either. If the prosecution successfully indicts (and, as the author

Tom Wolfe so famously put it, a decent prosecutor can get a ham sandwich indicted), then expect to go to trial, spend several hundred thousand dollars in the process, and burn through months to years of your life; all the while with a possible murder conviction hanging over your head and your entire future in doubt.

And then there's the jury. The jurors will know less about your case, even at the trial's conclusion, than nearly everybody else involved. The process carefully controls what facts are presented to them. There is a great deal of information known to you, and to the lawyers, and the judge, and the general public for that matter, that the jury will never hear before they render a verdict.

Even if the jury of your peers was given all the evidence favorable to you, that doesn't mean they'll see it that way. If you ever have the misfortune to be present during a jury selection process, you'll get a keen sense that some of your purported "peers" don't have the collective IQ of a household thermometer. They also are shockingly susceptible to a prosecutor's tale of wrongdoing. You do not want to place your life in the hands of such people if you can avoid it.

Now, all those treacherous legal waters I just described still assume that everyone is fair and impartial. That is not always the case. A "good bust" can get a cop a promotion; a large investigation can make a detective the next chief. Prosecutors routinely use their position to advance to political office, and those who are elected are politicians already.

What better way to get favorable press coverage, and lots of it, than to take a big case involving violence? So what if the evidence is a bit wishy-washy around the edges? Even the judge, accustomed to dealing only with local matters, may enjoy that sweet 15 minutes of national attention more than you find comfortable.

And it could get even worse than just unfair. Much worse. What if your case raises these people's political returns beyond anything they could have imagined? What if it provides them with a once-in-a-lifetime opportunity for career advancement? What if, for example, your attacker was someone of a different race than your own? The entire criminal justice process could become racially energized, to the considerable detriment of your due process rights.

I just painted a very scary portrait of the criminal justice system. The good news is that you can do something to greatly minimize your legal risk: Don't look vulnerable.

If an arrest isn't worth the paperwork, it often won't happen.

Once the investigation is done, if your case looks fruitless, resources will be assigned to more promising targets. After all, many prosecutors have a conviction rate well above 90% because they don't pursue cases they don't think they'll win.

To avoid being picked as a prosecutor's pet case, you want to look as legally invulnerable to successful prosecution as possible. Even one red flag of weakness in your case will attract prosecution like blood in the water will attract a shark.

So how does one avoid the "red flags"?

Obey the law and be prepared with a compelling story of innocence.

Sounds simple, right? And yet it's not actually that simple. The challenge is knowing what the laws you need to follow say, and then how to make your story of innocence match those laws.

I've designed this book to provide an understanding of the foundational principles you must understand if you are to understand self-defense law at all.

In this book we cover the five fundamental elements of a self-defense claim: innocence, imminence, proportionality, avoidance, and reasonableness. As I go along, I give lots of examples where people found themselves in trouble with each of these principles and show you what went wrong.

Then, I show how to make this knowledge of these five elements actionable by illustrating how they can guide you in developing a legally-sound self-defense strategy. This knowledge will help you position yourself so you can effectively and quickly apply what you learned in this book during the stress of the fight.

The ultimate goal is to help you develop your own personalized, and legally-sound, self-defense strategy that, to the greatest extent possible, improves your odds of winning both the physical and legal fight.

The final chapter of this book, "Learn More," will provide you with links to further resources you can take advantage of to further develop your understanding of self-defense law and how it's applied to real people in real cases of self-defense. These resources cover both use-of-force law generally, as well as state-specific statutes, court decisions, and jury instructions.

Those additional resources also expand beyond the scope of this "Principles" book to cover vital subjects like defense of others, defense of property, interacting with the police, consciousness of guilt evidence, and much more.

And if you're a self-defense or firearms instructor, you'll find a link to the Law of Self Defense Instructor Program, to our knowledge the most in-depth instruction available anywhere on use-of-force law—and that includes far more comprehensive instruction than what, to my knowledge, is provided in any law school.

There are things this book will not do. It will not teach you how to hurt or kill someone and then hide behind a facade of self-defense. If you are looking for a way to "game" the legal system for such purposes, you will be sorely disappointed.

This book will also not turn you into a lawyer. After reading it, you will almost certainly know far more about self-defense law than most lawyers you run into. But preparing and presenting an effective legal defense requires more than just an understanding of self-defense law.

The laws governing evidence and criminal procedure alone take intense study and years of practice, and can make or break a use-of-force case all by themselves.

Equally important are the particular facts of your case and the personalities of the prosecutor, judge, and jury. All these are part of the legal arts that only a skilled and experienced criminal defense lawyer has mastered.

One last note: It should go without saying that nothing in this book constitutes legal advice, but we live in a madly litigious society so I'll say it anyway: nothing in this book constitutes legal advice. Self-defense claims depend heavily on the facts of a case, and it is impossible for any general guide to replace the counsel a competent lawyer can provide.

To paraphrase the medical profession, should this be an emergency, hang up and dial a competent lawyer in the relevant jurisdiction. But it may be useful to bring this book with you to their office, so that you're an informed consumer of that lawyer's advice.

Chapter 1

Legal Principles & Processes

Before we dive into the deep end of the pool, we need a working knowledge of the criminal justice system, the "machine" that will consume you with ruthless inefficiency should you make a misstep. I like to think of our system as if it were a sports field, where you will play the highest stake game of your life . The game is unwinnable unless you know where the goalposts are, how goals (convictions) are scored, and how they're blocked (acquittal).

Competing Narratives

The startling truth about our system, which takes innocent people by surprise every day, is that it doesn't base its decisions on what actually happened. The quicker you realize your actions won't be judged on absolute reality, the quicker you can get ahead in the game.

This isn't a knock on the system. It's impossible for the people who will judge you to know what really happened, in any absolute sense, for the simple reason that they weren't there when it happened. Absent absolute knowledge, they're forced to base their conclusions on what the available evidence suggests probably happened.

This means the game is a competition between two stories, built around that available evidence. The prosecution will tell a story of guilt. They will paint a picture of you and your actions in the worst possible light to convince the jury that you broke the law. They will say your claim to innocence is flawed, you should be denied the legal defense of self-defense, and you should be held criminally liable. And make no mistake—they're in it to win.

Your defense counsel, on the other hand, will tell a story of innocence. They'll work to convince the jury that your actions were lawful, that your claim to innocence is true, that your legal defense of self-defense meets every legal condition required, and that your actions should, therefore, be found legally justified and you should be found free of legal liability.

These two stories—the narrative of guilt and the narrative of innocence—are all that a jury will have to go on.

Even long before the trial, the prosecutors and the defense counsel will pave the way to telling their competing stories. Each side will search for evidence that will hurt or help them. Each side will develop a sense of how strong or weak their story is likely to be relative to the other side's story. This process will start the moment the prosecutor gets your investigative file and the moment your lawyer's phone rings with your call.

So what is it that both sides are looking for? They need evidence that strengthens their stories in five fundamental ways—the five legal elements that are the key to a claim of self-defense. These five elements are: Innocence, Imminence, Proportionality, Avoidance, and Reasonableness.

Those five elements define all self-defense claims. They are also cumulative. Every element must be present for you to win (unless an element is legally waived for some reason, and then it's no longer required). You can think of them as five links in a chain from which your liberty is hanging. If even one of those links breaks, the chain breaks, and your claim fails. Period.

That means that in order for a prosecutor to defeat your claim of self-defense, he doesn't have to defeat it entirely—he need merely defeat any one of the required elements. If he does that, your claim of self-defense collapses entirely.

We will discuss each of the five elements of a self-defense claim in great detail in the next five chapters. For now, simply remember that the loss of any one of these five elements dooms your case.

With that in mind, it's time to understand how these elements are proven in a court of law, and who proves them.

Standards of Proof

A "standard of proof" is the amount of evidence needed for a jury to find you guilty. For our purposes here, there are two relevant standards: proof by a preponderance of the evidence and proof beyond a reasonable doubt.

Preponderance of the Evidence

Proof by a preponderance of the evidence means that it is more likely than not that a certain story is true. I like to think of this as 50% plus the slightest smidgeon. This standard of proof is the norm in civil court cases, where one party is suing another. Whichever side has the slightest majority of the evidence on their side is deemed the "winner."

What you might not know is that "by a preponderance of the evidence" can also play a role in self-defense law. Many states say juries may legally presume that a defendant facing an unlawful and forcible intruder in their home has a reasonable fear of imminent deadly force harm—in effect giving the defender most of what he needs to be lawfully justified in using deadly force against that intruder.

Such presumptions, though, can be overcome by a preponderance of the evidence. The presumption can be lost if, for example, the prosecution can convince the jury that it's more likely than not that the defendant staged the "break-in."

Preponderance of the evidence also shows up as a common standard of evidence in the context of self-defense immunity laws. These are laws that protect you from arrest, prosecution, and civil suits if you were lawfully defending yourself. But how does the system know your actions were innocent before the trial?

Answer: they hold a pre-trial immunity hearing. Whoever convinces the judge that they have a preponderance of the evidence on their side will win the immunity argument. If the defense wins, you are granted immunity and go free. If the prosecution wins, immunity is denied, and the parties prepare for trial.

Beyond a Reasonable Doubt

The standard of proof relevant to a claim of self-defense itself is proof beyond a reasonable doubt. This is a phrase all Americans have heard mentioned thousands of times in courtroom dramas on TV.

The criminal justice system recognizes that no jury can ever arrive at a verdict with 100% confidence. After all, they weren't there. They are relying on the carefully screened evidence of the case presented to them in court in order to inform them about what happened. But witnesses can lie and evidence can mislead.

Because no juror can be 100% certain, society accepts a lower level of confidence. In American criminal courts this lower but acceptable degree of certainty is called "beyond a reasonable doubt." If a juror, after listening to all the evidence and arguments in court, still has a reasonable doubts that the defendant committed the crime, then they must acquit (which means find the defendant "not guilty").

You might wonder what "beyond a reasonable doubt" really means. Ninety-nine percent confidence? Eighty percent? For better or worse, we've never come up with any more specific explanation than the phrase itself: "beyond a reasonable doubt." It's up to each juror to decide for themselves what this means.

I will say, though, that the words "reasonable doubt" provide some useful guidance all on their own. The US Supreme Court made a good illustration of their facets:

> "A reasonable doubt [is] one based on reason which arises from the evidence or lack of evidence."
>
> *Jackson v. Virginia,* 443 US 307 (US Supreme Court 1979)

Note the italicized terms: reason and evidence. A juror must apply their powers of reason to the evidence presented at trial, in accordance with the instructions they receive from the judge.

Reasonable doubt, then, cannot be based on mere speculation or imagination. There must be evidence from which a jury makes reasoned inferences.

I emphasize this because it's very common for uninformed people to do precisely what the law does not permit them to do—be prepared to use force against a speculative or imagined threat.

Here's a typical example of such a scenario: two people are discussing what they would do in a self-defense situation. Suddenly one of them justifies some defensive action by saying, "Well, for all I know, he could have a gun, or he could have a knife."

If there is evidence from which one can reasonably infer the guy has a gun or a knife—for example, he tells you that he does, or he makes a motion as if for a weapon, or he has a reputation for being armed at all times—that is a valid argument to make in court.

The phrase "for all I know," though, makes the gun or knife hypothetical. Speculative. Imaginary. And no legally valid conclusion can be based on the hypothetical, speculative, or imaginary.

OK, now that we know the two important standards of proof in a self-defense case—by a preponderance of the evidence and beyond a reasonable doubt—let's take a look at who must prove (or disprove) what.

Burdens of Proof

While standards of proof define how much evidence is needed, burdens of proof decide which side must produce and argue the evidence of a particular issue.

Just as we've all heard the phrase "beyond a reasonable doubt," we've all also heard the phrase "burden of proof." But what you may not know is that the burden of proof consists of two distinct facets: the "burden of production" and the "burden of persuasion." We'll discuss each of them in turn.

Burden of Production

You do not have an automatic right to tell a jury you acted in self-defense. Yes, you read that correctly.

If you want to be able to argue "self-defense" before a jury, there must be some actual evidence that you were defending yourself. And the responsibility for introducing that evidence into the courtroom, called the burden of production, falls squarely on you. If you fail to meet this burden, the jury will learn all about a dead "victim" and all about the gun that killed him in your hand, but not a single word about self-defense. Needless to say, getting this into court is imperative to your acquittal.

Fortunately, the burden of production is usually very low. If there is any evidence, however contested it might be, you will almost certainly be allowed to argue self-defense. In most cases of "good guy" self-defense there is little difficulty in meeting the burden of production.

Where people get into trouble is when they obviously violate one of the five required elements of a claim of self-defense. Say, for example, that you started the fight, and you admit it to the judge, meaning you've violated the required element of Innocence (which we cover in detail in the next chapter). If your state says that you can't start a fight and still claim self-defense, you simply can't meet your burden of production on the element of Innocence, and thus can't meet your burden of production on self-defense generally.

The prosecution also has its own burden of production. They are required to present evidence that you committed the crime with which you're charged. If they fail to meet this burden of production, which is usually argued before a grand jury, they won't be permitted to take you to trial at all.

That said, it is not typically difficult for a prosecutor to meet their burden of production in a self-defense case, because if you're claiming self-defense you've already admitted that you intentionally used force against that other guy. Whether that force was lawful or not is precisely the question to be settled at trial.

Assuming both sides have met their burden of production, such that both the criminal charge and the legal defense of self-defense can be argued at trial, it is time to proceed to the burden of persuasion.

Burden of Persuasion

For every issue in a trial, one side or the other bears the responsibility to prove (or disprove) that issue to some standard of evidence.

On the matter of the criminal charge, you are innocent until the prosecution persuades the jury beyond a reasonable doubt that you committed the crime. If the prosecution fails to meet this burden, the jury is told they must acquit you of the criminal charge.

Self-defense cases are no different from generic criminal cases in this respect. After all, if you're claiming self-defense, it's because you are charged with a use-of-force crime (e.g., murder, assault, etc.). The prosecution must first prove you committed that alleged unlawful act, or they lose before self-defense is even relevant. Why? Because if they fail to prove the underlying act, there's no need for the jury to even think about self-defense—you're simply not guilty of the crime charged, period, and don't need a legal defense.

Again, this is not a difficult task for the prosecution in a self-defense case. You already admitted to using force to defend yourself. You've already said, "Yes, I shot that person, and yes, they died as a result—but I did so in lawful self-defense." Once you say that, there's no doubt that the prosecution will easily meet the conditions for conviction... unless that conviction is stopped by a successful claim of self-defense.

So, on the criminal charge the prosecution bears both the burden of production to get the charge (and you) into court in the first place, as well as the burden of persuasion to convince the jury beyond a reasonable doubt that the elements of the charge have been proven.

What about on the legal defense of self-defense? We've already seen that for the legal defense, it is the defendant (you) who bears the burden of production. Assuming that's been accomplished, do you also bear the burden of persuasion on the issue of self-defense?

The answer, in all 50 states, is no. Every state places the burden of persuasion on self-defense on the prosecution, and to the legal standard of beyond a reasonable doubt. That is, the prosecution must disprove you acted in self-defense beyond a reasonable doubt. If they fail to meet this burden, the jury will be instructed to acquit you of the criminal charge.

It is hard to overemphasize how huge this is for the defendant in a self-defense case.

The prosecution could easily convince the jury that it's more likely than not that you did not act in self-defense. But that's not enough to overcome a claim of self-defense.

The prosecution could convince the jury that it's highly likely that you did not act in self-defense. But that's still not enough to overcome a claim of self-defense.

Unless the prosecution can convince the jury that you did not act in self-defense beyond a reasonable doubt, you must be acquitted.

To put it another way, as long as your defense counsel can maintain at least a reasonable doubt in the minds of the jury, an acquittal is yours.

Now, this sounds like a very heavy burden on the state. And it is. Yet prosecutors manage to defeat self-defense claims all the time. How is this possible? There are two factors that help prosecutors overcome this heavy burden.

First, they don't need to disprove every element of the claim of self-defense. They only need to disprove one element. And it is usually the decision-making and conduct of the defendant—that's you—that provides the evidence the prosecution needs to accomplish this mission. Through ignorance or mistake, it is usually the defendant that provides the prosecutor with that vulnerable element to target and destroy, and thus overcome the legal defense of self-defense and achieve a conviction.

That's on us. It is our responsibility to ensure that our use of force stays well within the rules so that we do not appear as vulnerable targets of prosecution. Indeed, this is a key mission of this book: to teach you how to minimize your legal vulnerability as close to zero as possible—to be hard to convict.

Not by learning "legal tricks"—we don't teach legal tricks. Rather by learning where the actual legal boundaries of self-defense really are, enabling you to stay well within those boundaries. Do that, and you'll be hard to convict, indeed.

The Criminal Justice Pipeline

At this point, I want to take a few moments to describe the criminal justice "pipeline" from the initial 911 call to conviction and beyond. I will describe a representative process, and the details will vary from jurisdiction to jurisdiction. Also, it's not uncommon for many steps to be skipped entirely—plea bargains or having charges dismissed are good examples of this.

Report of the Crime

To get the ball rolling down the criminal justice pipeline, someone must report a crime. You might have called the police, your attacker or a witness could have called, or (far less common) a police officer could have observed the encounter directly. If it is possible to report it yourself first, especially in a deadly force defensive use-of-force case, that's generally advisable.

Pre-Arrest Investigation

The police will (eventually) respond to the report of a crime and begin a preliminary investigation. This can be as simple as asking you, perhaps the other person (e.g., your attacker), perhaps witnesses, a few questions to figure out what happened. Or, teams of detectives and forensic scientists may descend on the scene and drape "crime scene" tape everywhere and comprehensively canvass the area for evidence and witnesses.

Arrest

If probable cause of a crime is found, congratulations—
you are now a "suspect" and will be arrested if the crime
is a serious one. For less serious crimes, like simple
assault, you may simply be issued a summons to appear
in court at a future date and released on your own
recognizance (your mere promise to show up at court).

In cases of homicide, an arrest is nearly certain if there
are no immunity provisions against it, so be prepared to
be arrested. It doesn't necessarily mean they'll keep you
on ice long. It may be that they just want to keep an eye
on you while they are gathering the first round of
information.

The legal definition of an arrest is that the police will
"seize you" and "take you into custody." If you are not
certain if you are under arrest, ask the police if you may
go. If you may, you are almost certainly under arrest
(although there are other grounds on which officers can
temporarily detain you without that constituting an
actual arrest).

If arrested, expect to be handcuffed and put in a secure
location, such as the back of a patrol car. You'll also
eventually be read your Miranda rights, and asked if you
understand them. As we all know, anything you say can
and may be used against you in court.

Booking

Once arrested, you will be transported to a police station to be "booked." This is literally police bookkeeping. They will photograph and fingerprint you, and perhaps take a cheek-swab DNA sample. They will confiscate and inventory your possessions. You may receive a more detailed description of the charges against you than what you were told at the scene. And, of course, you get your one phone call.

People sometimes ask me for my business card so that they have a lawyer they can call after being arrested. Frankly, I think the benefit of having some lawyer's card in your wallet is overstated. Lawyers usually work 9-5 Monday through Friday and are often in court even then. Self-defense encounters more often occur in the hours of darkness. Call your lawyer at o-dark-thirty, and they probably won't answer the phone. Also, when was the last time you even spoke to that lawyer whose card you're carrying? When he did your house closing 10 years ago?

Instead, I recommend that you call someone who keeps their cell on them, will take your call, and will work hard on your behalf once you hang up. Do you have family members who doesn't go out much? They're a good choice. A wife you know is home? A business partner? Your next-door neighbor? Any of those people can call your lawyer and others on your behalf while you're making new and interesting friends in your jail cell.

Post-Arrest Investigation

Although your arrest means that the officers on the scene believe that there's enough evidence for probable cause, it's evidence "beyond a reasonable doubt" that will be required to convict you, and that's a much higher standard.

Police will conduct a post-arrest investigation to find the evidence needed to meet that burden of persuasion of beyond a reasonable doubt. That post-arrest investigation could be very brief. A few conversations with witnesses while you are being driven to the police station may be enough. On the other hand, some investigations can last for months. If successful, the evidence that investigators compile is put in an investigative report and sent to the state prosecutor's office.

Decision to Charge

When your investigative report hits the prosecutor's desk, they'll have to decide whether there's enough evidence for a conviction. This is a judgment call that's essentially entirely within their discretion.

Prosecutors are "graded" on their win-loss record, so they won't usually bother with a losing case. Bad cases are not a good use of the taxpayer's money when many other potentially more promising cases await attention.

If prosecutors believe that they don't have enough evidence to convict, they may still pretend that they do have such evidence a ruse to threaten a trial and get you to agree to a plea bargain or some sort of pre-trial diversion scheme. That's perfectly lawful.

Alternatively, they may decide the matter is not worth pursuing and kick you loose, dismissing the case outright. Keep in mind, though, that if they find more evidence later, they can pick you back up.

The Complaint

If prosecutors decide to try you, the prosecutor will file a criminal complaint in the lowest-level court, called the magistrate court. For lower-level offenses such as misdemeanors, the magistrate may deal with the whole matter. Felony offenses begin here but are then brought to the next higher-level court for the actual trial.

The criminal complaint is a description of the crime charged and a sworn statement from police describing the evidence that aligns with each of the elements of that criminal charge. The magistrate will review the complaint, but this is usually a rubber-stamp process.

Arraignment

Once the magistrate accepts the complaint, you officially graduate from being a "suspect" to a "defendant." The magistrate will tell you the official charge against you, ask if you understand the charge, and ask for a plea. By now you should definitely have a lawyer, but if you don't, under no circumstances are you to say anything else but "not guilty." No. Matter. What. Nothing bad can come from pleading "not guilty," and it maximizes your options moving forward.

Also, do not argue your case to the magistrate; it's not their job to judge the case, and anything you say can and may be used against you at a later trial. Be polite and say,

"Yes, your Honor," "No, your Honor," and "Not guilty, your Honor." That's it.

Next, the magistrate court will decide bail. Depending on the circumstances, they might release you on your own recognizance, meaning simply on your promise to return when required.

Alternatively, they could set a bail amount, varying from a few hundred to a few million dollars. The bail serves as an incentive to get you to come back. If you don't show, the court will keep your money.

They may also impose conditions of bail, such as house arrest, wearing an ankle bracelet, turning over your firearms to law enforcement, and pretty much whatever other conditions the court may wish to impose.

If the crime you're charged with is very severe, or if they think you are a high risk of flight (a no-show in court), they may simply deny bail and make you wait in jail until your trial.

Grand Jury (or Equivalent) & Indictment

After the arraignment, the prosecutors will have to "qualify" you for criminal trial, usually with a grand jury, or alternatively by a sworn document called an "information" (states differ on this step). At this stage, only the prosecution introduces evidence. The defense may challenge the evidence produced by the prosecution, but is generally not permitted to introduce evidence of their own.

A grand jury's purpose is to answer the question, "Absent a defense, would the defendant be convicted?" If the answer is "no," if the prosecution cannot win even without an opposing argument, then there's no chance they'll win with one. In practice, though, this is another rubber-stamp step, and a formal indictment is returned.

Pre-trial Motions

The last step before trial is the pretrial period, including pretrial motions. This may all sound preliminary, administrative, and unimportant, but make no mistake. This is where the stage and rules of the trial are set, meaning this is where the legal battlefield is defined. This period can last months, and you may well wish you had more of it.

Modern legal battles have unique rules. Some of these are fixed and identical for every trial, but others may vary based on the facts of the case. Your future can easily be decided on whether these rules are set in your favor. In short, the trial is often effectively won or lost before it even starts, in the defining of this legal battlefield.

During this period, your defense team will scour the evidence for weaknesses in the prosecutor's case, as well as identify evidence and resources like expert witnesses to flesh out the theory of the case they'll present at trial—presumably, given the context of this book, the legal defenses of self-defense.

This is also the phase where the judge decides what evidence will be permitted into trial and what evidence will be excluded, and whether you may argue self-defense at all. That is to say, this is the stage where your lawyer must meet your burden of production to argue self-defense.

Around this time, you'll really start to appreciate the creativity, expertise, and experience of your lawyer, or deeply regret the lack of the same. Good lawyers are expensive. You might someday regret paying a good lawyer tons of money, but you'll almost certainly regret paying little for a bad one.

Once the judge allows or denies all the pretrial motions, and the shape of the battlefield has been defined, it is time for the last step before opening statements: jury selection.

Jury Selection

Jury selection is the ultimate wildcard. Trials are tightly controlled affairs, with the judge wielding great power to allow or restrain lawyers on each side.

But the jury is something else. They sit there completely silent, listening and thinking, and ultimately deciding your fate. But who are these people? Your peers? Do they share your worldview, your cultural view, and your particular life experiences?

Of course not. They are only your "peers" in the sense that they are subject to being called for jury service just like you. In all other respects, they are a black box. Unknown.

So your lawyer (and the state's lawyers) will question the jurors in a process called voir dire. They'll try to identify and exclude people who have already formed an opinion of the case. The theoretical goal is to get a jury of people who can all be fair and impartial, and who will consider only the evidence presented at trial and not "facts" they may have heard from friends, family, or media sources outside the courtroom.

Naturally, if either side believes they have an opportunity to tilt the makeup of the jury in their favor, they are sure to try to take advantage of it.

As with the pretrial hearings, jury selection can decide the trial's outcome before it starts. Unlike the pretrial hearings, picking the right juror over the wrong one is an uncertain effort. That's why competent jury consultants get paid the big bucks.

Trial

The trial consists of six major components: opening statements, the prosecution's presentation of the case, the defendant's presentation of the case, closing arguments, jury instructions, and deliberation.

In opening statements each side outlines their story and explains that over the course of the trial they will tell that story in detail, supported by facts in evidence.

Both the prosecution and the defense become storytellers, using the evidence as raw material to construct those stories. They are each free to choose or ignore evidence, or interpret a given piece of evidence differently, but they must both draw from the same pool of evidence.

Both sides know all the evidence before the trial starts because of what's called "mandatory mutual discovery." Unlike courtroom dramas, there is no evidence "ambushes" in real trials.

The prosecution is the first to speak. This is a powerful advantage because they get to paint the first picture in the jurors' heads. Only then will the defense outline their "story" for the jury.

After opening statements, the prosecution presents its case. They will show the jury evidence and witness testimony through what is called "direct" questioning. After the prosecution has finished with each witness, the defense can ask them questions in "cross-examination." Once they're done, if the prosecution wishes, it can come back and re-direct, the defense can re-cross, and so on. This cycle continues until both sides are finished.

When the prosecution is done presenting all its evidence, it will "rest" its case. Now it is the defense team's turn. This is the mirror image of the prosecution's side of things, with an important difference.

The prosecution needs to argue effectively enough to prove its case beyond a reasonable doubt on each aspect of the charge. But the defense only needs to create a reasonable doubt. For this reason, your team may ignore many points argued by the prosecution, instead focusing on the single chink that can unravel the criminal charge.

The defense can even elect to present no defense whatever, and let the matter go straight to the jury. (Of course, this is rarely done, as it tends to make defendants think they paid too much for their lawyer.)

Regardless of how long it takes, when the defense rests its case, it is time for closing arguments.

Each side once again tells their story in closing, this time emphasizing the particular bits and pieces of evidence that strengthen them and undermine their adversary. And once again, the prosecutors get the better slot. While they spoke first in opening statements, they speak last in closing arguments. So the first and last thing the jury hears is the prosecutor's story. Once closing arguments are done, it is time for jury instruction and deliberation.

Jury Instruction and Deliberation

The jurors are not legal experts. To help them with their job, the court gives them both oral and written instructions. Although many states now have a set of standard jury instructions, each side may suggest modifications that will, naturally, favor their desired outcome. Just as pretrial rulings defined the battlefield of the trial, motions from both sides on the jury instructions can define the battlefield in the jury room.

Once the jury has their instructions, they are sent into isolation for their deliberations. Most states use 12 person juries for felonies, some use 6, but in either case the jury must unanimously agree before they can return a verdict. If a unanimous verdict cannot be reached, the jury is "hung," and a mistrial declared.

Sentencing

If the jury decides the defendant is guilty, the next stage is sentencing. Here the judge considers a great deal of evidence that wasn't available to the jury, such as the defendant's prior criminal convictions. The judge may also consider mitigating factors.

Most often, though, the law determines the sentence within some broad range, and the judge's discretion is limited to that range. Some crimes also require a mandatory minimum sentence (e.g., Florida's "10-20-Life" gun crime sentencing scheme), where the judge has no discretion in sentencing.

Appeals

After the trial, the defendant may appeal a conviction to an intermediate "appellate" court of usually three judges. Those judges may spend only a few minutes on your case before rejecting the appeal because of the enormous number of cases coming across their desk.

If they do accept the appeal, though, the judges will carefully decide how the laws, but not the facts, were applied at trial. They avoid reconsidering facts because they were not at trial to observe the testimony and evidence directly. Instead ,they ensure that the law was applied properly and fairly. The appellate court can affirm a conviction, reverse a conviction, or decide just about anything in between (e.g., reduce a murder conviction to manslaughter).

If the appellate court affirms the verdict, you may appeal to your state's Supreme Court. This court, though, takes on only very few cases at their sole discretion. It is the rare criminal defendant whose case is heard before their state's Supreme Court. As with the appellate court, they can affirm, reverse, or decide just about anything in between.

The Crime Charged

Now that we better know the process, we should spend a few minutes on what you'll be charged with if you have to defend yourself. The charges you face define what the prosecution will have to prove and the consequences if you are found guilty.

The statutes and jury instructions for these crimes in all 50 states can be found at the Law of Self Defense website: lawofselfdefense.com.

Murder

Murder is the unlawful, deliberate, and premeditated killing of a human with what some jurisdictions call a "depraved mind."

Murder has degrees, the most serious being murder in the first degree, or capital murder in states having the death penalty. Usually, it involves some serious aggravating factor such as killing a police officer, a child, or some other protected person. One can also qualify because of the "heinous" nature of the murder, such as torture. First-degree murder is usually punishable by life imprisonment without possibility of early release or even death (in capital punishment states).

Murder in the second degree is what most of us think of as common murder—murder for insurance money or to dispatch a hated business competitor. "Murder 2" is usually sentenced with 20 years to life.

Murder needs to be distinguished from "homicide," which is the taking of another human life. Such taking may be legal, such as in lawful self-defense. Only if the taking of life was illegal does it qualify as murder.

Manslaughter

Manslaughter comes in two forms: voluntary and involuntary. Voluntary manslaughter happens when you meant to harm someone but didn't deliberately plan to take their life, or act against them with a "depraved mind." The classic example is a husband who finds his wife in bed with another man, and kills one or both of them.

Involuntary manslaughter happens when you don't mean to cause harm, but death still occurred because of criminal negligence. Killing someone while drunk driving is a classic example. Involuntary manslaughter is not relevant to self-defense, because self-defense always involves a deliberate decision to act.

Manslaughter calls for about 15 years in jail, but the sentence can be much lower or much higher depending on the circumstances and aggravating factors (e.g., use of a deadly weapon). It is often a lesser-included offense of murder, meaning a murder trial jury can still convict on manslaughter even if the state fails to prove the higher threshold of murder.

Assault

Assault is the first of the non-homicide charges. You commit assault when you put someone in fear of immediate physical harm. The type of threat determines whether it is simple assault—you put someone in fear of your bare hands—or aggravated assault—you put someone in fear of your handgun. Simple assault carries a sentence of a few months or a few years in jail, but aggravated assault can be very serious with sentences as great as 15 years.

Battery

Battery is the unwanted and deliberate touching of another person. As with assault, it can be either simple battery—you hit somebody with non-deadly force—or aggravated battery—you hit them with deadly force. The prospective punishments are the same as for assault: a few months or years in jail for simple battery, and up to 15 years for aggravated battery.

Assault and battery may stand alone, or may be combined, depending on the circumstances. If you wave your fist in someone's face but do not touch him or her, you committed assault but not battery. If you strike someone's backside but they were never aware of the attack coming, you have committed battery but not assault, because they can't be afraid of what they didn't know was coming. Of course, if your oncoming attack makes them afraid and you make contact, you have committed classic assault and battery.

It's also the case that some states apply the terms assault and battery somewhat differently or interchangeably, so it's important to understand the underlying elements of the actual criminal charge rather than just rely on the label given.

Brandishing

When you show a dangerous weapon in a rude, angry, or threatening way, you have committed brandishing. This charge can be expected when you pull your gun in self-defense, even if you don't use it. Given the court's increasing tendency to describe pepper spray and Tasers as dangerous weapons, though, showing them might also be characterized as brandishing.

Brandishing is typically a misdemeanor punished with a fine of several hundred dollars and a few weeks jail time. In some jurisdictions, though, brandishing is a felony when it's done in certain locations (e.g., near schools) or toward certain individuals (e.g., police officers).

Disorderly Conduct

Disorderly conduct is a "catch-all" charge for a wide variety of annoying behavior. Formally, conduct is disorderly if it causes an inconvenience, annoyance, or alarm. Expect this charge if you were publicly fighting, using grossly abusive language against someone (the 'N' word, for instance), getting in the way of someone's walking, insulting someone, or taunting them. Disorderly conduct typically results in a fine on the order of several hundred dollars and a month or two in jail.

The real danger of a disorderly conduct charge is when it's combined a something more serious, such as murder, like murder. If you get both, disorderly conduct will make you look bad, perhaps overly aggressive, and could prevent you from even arguing self-defense, and may make a jury perceive the murder charge as more credible than it would have looked absent the disorderly conduct charge.

Illegal Possession of a Concealed Weapon

There are thousands of laws, rules, and regulations at the local, state, and federal levels about what gun you can possess and where. These laws vary by state and within states.

Most jurisdictions require you to obtain a formal license to carry a concealed gun, but even with such a permit, there are places you still may not bring it. It is your responsibility to know the laws anywhere you may be and follow them. Ignorance of the law is not a defense.

The failure to adhere to these laws can fatally damage your self-defense claim. As with the disorderly conduct, illegally possessing a weapon can strip you of the required mantle of innocence that you need to argue self-defense.

The Legal Defense of Self-Defense

To all these criminal charges you can potentially raise the legal defense—that your use of force, normally unlawful, should be deemed justified because you were lawfully defending yourself.

Once you've met your burden of production on the legal defense of self-defense the burden of proof shifts to the prosecution to disprove your claim of self-defense beyond a reasonable doubt.

If the jury concludes that the state has failed to disprove self-defense beyond a reasonable doubt, they must acquit.

So the prosecution must not only first prove you "guilty" of the crime itself, but also prove that you did not act in self. Self-defense is, of course, what this book is all about, and we'll cover that subject in great detail. Before we do, however, I want to distinguish self-defense from accidental killing.

Accidental Killing

Accidental killing, unlike involuntary manslaughter, happens when you did something legal that you didn't believe would cause harm, but someone still died. Accidental killings are also an absolute defense.

An example of a genuine accident might be as follows. While traveling, you rent a car. Having only a small carry-on bag, you toss it on the passenger seat and drive away. Unknown to you, local gangsters have earlier tossed an unconscious bound-and-gagged competitor in the trunk of the car. While you're driving, carbon monoxide fills the trunk, asphyxiating the competitor. The following day you have the shocking experience of discovering the deceased in the trunk and notify the police.

Your actions were lawful, and your conduct would not raise any significant red flags. That's an accident in the legal sense, and the legal defense of accident, if successful, will hold you free of criminal liability.

Self-defense is the opposite of an accident. You do not intend an accident to happen. Self-defense is deliberate and intentional. You perceived a threat, and you purposely threatened or used force against that threat.

Self-defense and accident, then, are logically inconsistent. If your conduct was one, it cannot be the other.

I mention this because you must be careful not to confuse a self-defense narrative by saying the gun "just went off" or "I didn't mean for it to happen" or even explicitly "it was an accident," when really your use of force was genuine self-defense.

If you claim your use of force was an accident, or use words that can be interpreted as meaning it was an accident, you can seriously undermine your case. Indeed, you could eliminate any hope of meeting your burden of production in the first place. So, if you acted in self-defense, make sure you don't contradict yourself.

On the other hand, if your use of force was genuinely an accident, then you might need to raise the legal defense of accident in place of self-defense. The defense of accident, though, is rarely effective when applied to firearms cases because firearms are inherently dangerous instruments, and the standard of care for handling them is very high.

If you have a firearm and it discharges and injures someone, it is almost certain that the discharge and injury were the result of negligent handling. In the context of an inherently dangerous instrument, simple negligence can quickly become criminal negligence.

And, as we said earlier, criminal negligence that results in death is the definition of involuntary manslaughter.

Wrap-Up

None of the people who are judging the lawfulness (or not) of your actions were present when it happened. They are basing their conclusion on what the available evidence suggests might have happened.

From this evidence, two narratives, or stories, are built: a compelling narrative of guilt and a compelling narrative of innocence. These two narratives are all that the jury will have to go on in deciding your fate.

Both narratives will focus on the five essential elements of a self-defense claim: Innocence, Imminence, Proportionality, Avoidance, and Reasonableness. All required elements must be present, or a claim of self-defense fails.

A standard of evidence is the amount of evidence needed for a jury to make a decision. A "preponderance of the evidence" simply means a majority of the evidence.

A criminal trial requires the jury to believe "beyond a reasonable doubt" that the defendant committed the crime before they may convict. That is, the prosecution's case must have removed all reasonable doubt of guilt from the jurors' minds.

It is important that a reasonable doubt—and every conclusion arrived at in a trial—can not be based on mere speculation or imagination. It must be the result of the jurors' powers of reason applied to actual evidence in the case. Speculation and imagination are no basis for argument or conclusion at trial.

For those states that have immunity statutes, if there isn't at least a preponderance of the evidence that you behaved criminally, you'll be "kicked loose" from the system early, as well as perhaps enjoy protection from civil suit.

Whereas standards of proof define how much evidence must be presented to win on an issue, burdens of proof define which side is required to show and argue that evidence. There are two parts to the burden of proof: the burden of production and the burden of persuasion.

The burden of production defines who must provide the evidence to the court needed to raise the issue at trial in the first place. The State has the burden of production on the criminal charge. You have the burden to produce evidence of self-defense.

In most "good" self-defense cases the burden of production on self-defense is not hard to meet. If it is not met, however, the consequences are disastrous—the jury will never hear the words "self-defense" said at trial. This leads to an easy conviction because you already conceded to your use of force when you raised self-defense in the first place.

The burden of persuasion defines who has the responsibility of proving (or disproving) an issue to the jury, once the burden of production has been met.

This is a very heavy burden on the prosecution in a self-defense case, but two things make their job of overcoming self-defense easier. First, they do not need to disprove all the required elements of self-defense beyond a reasonable doubt, but only any one of them. Second, it is usually the defendant's poor decision-making and conduct that make it possible for the prosecution to meet their burden of persuasion.

The criminal justice system's "pipeline" begins with a report of the crime and a pre-arrest investigation. If the police think there is enough evidence, the "suspect" is arrested and booked. More investigation is conducted, and then the culmination of that effort is delivered to the district attorney's office, where they decide whether or not to prosecute. If they decide yes, they will file a complaint accusing you of a crime, and you will be arraigned. That is where you can plead "not guilty" and have bail set.

From here, a grand jury (or equivalent process) will decide whether the state's case, standing alone, would return a guilty verdict. If so, an indictment is handed down, and preparations begin in earnest for trial. Pretrial motions establish the ground rules of the trial and what evidence the jurors will be allowed to hear.

A jury will be selected in voir dire and a trial is conducted. If the result of juror deliberations is "guilty," you are sentenced and go to jail, though you may appeal the judgment to a higher circuit court. They will not reverse your trial decision by reconsidering the facts of your case, though. They will only decide whether what happened at trial was legally sound.

You could be charged with any of a variety of crimes if you use defensive force. The most likely charges are murder, manslaughter, aggravated assault & battery, or simple assault and battery.

Even if you didn't hurt someone, you could still be charged with brandishing, disorderly conduct, or illegal possession of a concealed weapon. These secondary charges, when added to a defensive force charge, can seriously undermine your self-defense claim.

There is also a legal defense of accident, and a genuine accident should carry no legal liability. In the context of firearms, however, the legal defense of accident is a difficult one. Guns are inherently dangerous instruments, and the legal standard of care is very high. Unintentional injuries or deaths involving guns are almost always the result of negligence, and in the context of a firearm, that usually constitutes criminal negligence.

Self-defense, if believed by the jury, is an absolute defense to all these charges and demands acquittal.

Chapter 2

Element 1: Innocence

A guy comes out of the darkness suddenly. You don't know him, but you must have done *something* to tick him off because he's barreling at you like an enraged bull yelling that he's going to kill you.

Just as he gets close enough for him to throw a punch at you, you swing to the side and trip him. He's on the ground for just a moment before he's back up and comes at you again.

You swing again, and this time you connect, but it's only a graze. He finally throws a punch of his own and misses as you knee him in the groin. He doubles over, and you know you're the victor.

Here's the problem. Later he says that you hit him first. Look back – he's right. He may have started things off by rushing at you, but you struck the first blow. Now, he says that all the punches *he* threw were to defend against *your* attack.

Still, surely *he* is the guilty party, not you. Right?

Right.

Our society has made self-defense legal in certain circumstances. This legal privilege, though, is reserved only for those who are deemed "innocent." Don't confuse this version of "innocent" with "innocent" versus "not guilty" at trial. This version of the word means you didn't start the conflict and is the first of the five principles of self-defense law.

In our example, the angry guy's behavior was clearly aggressive, and he has only himself to blame for your defensive response. In legal language, he is the "aggressor" and cannot claim self-defense to justify his actions, while your actions are legally justifiable self-defense because you were not the "aggressor."

Rather, you were the innocent victim of his aggression. In terms of the five elements of self-defense law, you've retained the key element of Innocence.

So how might you get into trouble in a court of law with regard to this element of Innocence? You lose Innocence if the prosecution can successfully argue that it was you who was the initial aggressor or provoked the fight. In other words, don't start, forcibly sustain, or escalate a fight.

You may have read this and thought, "Don't start the fight. What a no-brainer. This isn't something that I need to worry about—I don't go around starting fights."

If only life were so straightforward.

Who *really* started the fight is often not as clear-cut to the rest of the world as it is to you. The people deciding whether you started it will only have second-hand information. As a result, their conclusion will be based *solely* on the evidence available to them, and they will have to *infer* what might have happened.

Actually, in the case of the jurors, it is even worse than that. Their conclusion will be based on just the portion of the evidence that the court *allows* them to see, colored by the prosecution's and defense's spin, and applied only in ways permitted by the judge.

Whether the jurors think what happened was anything like what really happened is subject to factors not always in your control, at least not after the evidence is gathered. What matters is whether the prosecution can convince the jury that you provoked the conflict, not whether you actually provoked it.

So how might there be evidence that makes it look like you started, sustained, or escalated the conflict, even if you did not?

For one, there may be false eyewitness testimony. The penalties for lying under oath don't always stop bad people, and your attacker's friends could decide to testify that it was you, not he, who "started it."

Or, you could have done something, seemingly harmless at the time, which the prosecutor will magnify out of all proportion to make you look like the bad guy. Let's say you accidentally bumped into a guy, and he turned and attacked you. Could a prosecutor transform "accidentally bumped" into "aggressively shoved"? Don't put it past them.

Alternatively, you could have escalated the conflict's level of danger in a moment of panic. Even though you didn't start the fight, adding a knife to a fistfight is dangerous legal ground.

Finally, you could have a reputation in the community for being a "hothead," whether you are one or not. That doesn't mean you started this fight, but many juries are allowed to consider your reputation in the context of a self-defense case.

How Innocence is Lost

The question then is, "How can I better conduct myself so that everyone will perceive that I was not the aggressive person?" In other words, to minimize the chances that you'll be perceived as having lost the element of Innocence?

The answer to this begins with the definition of provocation. In order to be considered the "aggressive" party in a conflict, your actions must be legally deemed "sufficiently provocative." But what kinds of behaviors qualify?

The answer varies considerably from state to state. Luckily, the Federal courts have an elegant general definition. They define provocation as:

> "An *affirmative, unlawful* act reasonably *calculated to produce an affray* foreboding *injurious or fatal consequences.*"

That's a mouthful, but it combines a number of very useful concepts, which I have emphasized. Let's take a closer look at each one.

First, the act must be "affirmative." So an accident, say, unintentionally bumping into somebody, is not provocation.

Second, the behavior must be "unlawful," or if not itself unlawful then apparently intended towards an unlawful end. Using force to prevent someone from entering your home, then, is not aggressive behavior, because such conduct on your part is not unlawful.

Third, it must be "calculated to produce an affray." You must have a premeditated desire to create a physical conflict.

And fourth, the act must have the potential for "injurious or fatal consequences." The act must be intrinsically dangerous.

Unfortunately, self-defense cases are rarely in Federal court, and the states don't all agree with the Federal definition, let alone each other. So let's go through a few various ways states approach the problem of determining if someone has lost the element of Innocence.

Thresholds

Words Alone

In a few states, aggressive words alone may be sufficient to qualify as provocation and can cost you the element of Innocence—so saying anything threatening risks your claim of self-defense.

EXAMPLE CASE: *State v. Effler*
698 S.E.2d 547 (NC Ct. App. 2010)

James Effler, the defendant, lived with his girlfriend. He allowed an unemployed friend, Dan Brown, to temporarily stay with them, but after a time got frustrated with Brown for not getting a job and finding his own place.

On a November morning in 2007 Effler left a note for Brown saying that he would have to make other living arrangements and then left for his job site with his boss, Thomas Thompson. Brown found the note, got irritated, and yelled at Effler's girlfriend until she was in tears. She phoned her boyfriend, told him about Brown's behavior, and said she was not comfortable staying in the trailer alone with him. She asked Effler to come home, and he agreed. Others in the vehicle with him testified that Effler was worried and upset.

Effler got home and threw Brown's tools from the truck, shouting "here's your … tools if that's what you want." In response, Brown ran at the vehicle with a baseball bat, struck the vehicle's windshield, and poked the bat through the open driver's side window at Effler. It was obvious Brown and Effler were going to fight, so Thompson asked Brown to give him the bat, and Brown did. Brown and Effler then started in with their fists. At some point during the fistfight Effler grabbed the bat and struck Brown in the legs with it, putting Brown on the ground. Witnesses testified that throughout the fight Effler was shouting at Brown, "You should have just went—I told you to go the 'F' home. You should have just went home." Standing over Brown's now prone body, he said that "If [Brown] didn't stop he would double or triple his skull with [the bat]." Eventually one of the witnesses shouted to Effler that Brown had had enough, and pulled Effler away. The fight ended with Brown lying on the ground, grievously injured. Effler's girlfriend called law enforcement and emergency personnel to assist Brown, who was declared dead at the hospital.

Surprisingly, the autopsy revealed that Brown had been stabbed in the chest and back, including a stab that deeply penetrated his heart. Effler claimed self-defense. The court instructed the jury "the defendant would not be guilty ... if he acted in self-defense and was not the aggressor," that "if the defendant voluntarily ... entered the fight, he would be considered the aggressor," and that "one enters the fight voluntarily if he uses . . . abusive language which . . . [is] intended to bring on a fight." The jury found the defendant guilty of voluntary manslaughter, and the court sentenced him to 92 to 120 months of prison. He appealed.

The appellate court noted "[A]n individual is the aggressor if he aggressively and willingly enters into a fight without legal excuse or provocation. A person is considered to be an aggressor when he has provoked a present difficulty by language or conduct towards another that is calculated and intended to bring it about." They affirmed his conviction. Effler, then, stands as an example where words alone were sufficiently provocative.

Requirement of an Overt Act

For most states, threatening words alone are *not* enough to cost you your self-defense claim. Those words in combination with even the slightest physical aggression, however, could lose you the element of Innocence. The courts call this required physical conduct an *overt act*.

Indeed, in Commonwealth v. Mouzon the Pennsylvania Supreme Court found that just following someone around could constitute aggression if you are following them and using threatening words. This was held true even though the defendant in the case wasn't the first to use physical force.

EXAMPLE CASE: *Commonwealth v. Mouzon* 2012 Pa. LEXIS 1889 (PA Supreme Court 2012)

Darrin Mouzon, the defendant, spent several hours drinking in a Philadelphia bar. Shortly after midnight, he approached and tried to speak with two women who had just arrived with some friends. When the women turned down his advances and moved away from him, he pursued them through the bar, calling them rude names and threatening that he would "kill those bitches." The women and their companions decided to leave. As they were walking out, Mr. Mouzon angrily confronted them, and a man named King intervened.

King, a large man, punched Mouzon several times. Mouzon pulled a loaded gun from his waistband, and King threw his hands in the air and backed away. Mouzon fired twice. The first round hit a bystander in the leg, and the second struck King in the head, killing him. The trial court decided that Mouzon could not claim self-defense because he provoked the conflict (e.g., failed the element of innocence). Mouzon was convicted of murder and sentenced to life imprisonment. He appealed his conviction.

On appeal, Mouzon's lawyer argued that his "insulting and scandalous words" did not constitute provocation. Rather, he said King was the aggressor because King used physical force first. The defendant argued that the encounter "changed radically" when King accosted him over what had up to then been a "trivial matter" of non-physical harassment. He should, therefore, have been permitted to argue self-defense at trial.

The Pennsylvania Supreme Court rejected the defendant's arguments noting:

"In arguing self-defense, appellee would have his physical fight with the victim viewed in isolation, with the victim initiating the difficulty as the sole physical aggressor, and appellee acting in responsive self-defense. But, this is an incomplete and inaccurate view of the circumstances for self-defense purposes. The altercation between appellee and King did not occur spontaneously, or in isolation; it was the culmination of an ongoing confrontation in the bar initiated by appellee alone and continued and escalated by appellee alone. "

Specifically addressing Mouzon's argument that King was the first to use physical force and therefore was the aggressor, the Pennsylvania Supreme Court held that:

"Appellee is correct that there is decisional law suggesting that merely insulting or scandalous words of a light or trivial kind do not suffice to establish the requisite provocation to negate a claim of self-defense. But, the uncontested evidence here shows that appellee's words and actions were substantially more provocative than a mere verbal insult. Appellee did not simply utter rude or crass comments to the women; he closely followed the women down a flight of stairs, verbally haranguing them the entire time. Moreover, he threatened to kill them, in no uncertain terms. Not all words are the same; and words combined with conduct can be extremely provocative. Threats to kill, moreover, invite response or even interference, including from those with a sense of chivalry, and even from those of a mind to go further and punish the provocateur."

The Pennsylvania Supreme Court upheld the guilty verdict. Mouzon is a good example of where threatening words and even just slightly aggressive behavior qualified him as the aggressor, even when he did not start the physical fight.

Physical Force Alone

If there are no provocative words uttered, so we're limiting our considerations solely to actions, then it's the first person to use or threaten physical force who is the initial aggressor in the fight.

This is not necessarily the person who fired the first shot or who struck the first blow. You are not required to let your attacker "go first" before you can defend yourself.

All that is required for them, rather than you, to be the aggressor is that their hit was *about* to happen (we'll discuss this in the context of the element of Imminence in greater detail in the next chapter).

Keep in mind, though, that police, prosecutors, judges, and jurors will all tend to see the person who got the first blow in as the one who provoked the conflict unless you can convince them otherwise. If you strike first, you will need to have a well-articulated explanation for why it was necessary to do so.

Pursuit / Sustaining a Fight

Please don't sustain or "re-kindle" a fight. Even if the other person started the first round, if the fight ends but you start in again, you will be blamed for starting a second conflict. You will have become the aggressor in a second fight, and lost self-defense for that second fight. One of the most common ways people lose the element of Innocence is when a "defender" pursues an attacker or leaves and then comes back to the confrontation.

EXAMPLE CASE: *State v. Makidon*
2008 Minn. App. Unpub. LEXIS 357 (MN Ct. App. 2008)

Charles Makidon was annoyed with a neighbor's barking dog and walked next door to complain. He found the neighbor's children playing outside and gave them an earful. Their parents, later hearing of this, came by Makidon's house to discuss the matter, meeting Makidon at his front door.

Makidon later testified that his neighbors threatened him. In response, he went into his house and returned with a revolver. The neighbors, seeing the gun, prudently retreated and called the police.

Makidon was tried and convicted of the reckless use of a dangerous weapon and attempted discharge of a firearm. He appealed his conviction on the basis that it was his neighbor, not him, who had provoked the conflict. The appellate court noted that regardless of who was the aggressor in the initial argument, "when Makidon retreated into his home, rather than simply closing and locking the door, he returned with a revolver, an act of aggression." Essentially, any provocation by the neighbors in the conflict had been—or should have been—resolved when Makidon retreated safely into his home. Returning armed to confront his neighbors was starting a second conflict. Makidon's conviction was affirmed.

Mutual Combat

Mutual combat is another common way to lose the element of Innocence. In mutual combat, the parties agree, either explicitly or implicitly, to engage in a physical confrontation. The classic example is the "let's take this outside and settle it like men" scenario. When these men subsequently take it outside and engage in mutual combat, both are seen as initial aggressors and neither behaved legally. Genuine self-defense only happens when one party starts the fight against the wishes of the other.

We are all most vulnerable to being considered a mutual combatant when we have a long-standing grievance with our attacker. A bad neighbor, an argumentative coworker, or the girlfriend's ex-con boyfriend who can't let her go are all good examples of this. These are the types of fights a prosecutor, armed with some ambivalent facts, will gleefully try to sell to the jury as mutual combat.

It is important, then, to keep a level head with such frustrating people. Argumentative or even threatening words can later be recounted to your detriment. On the flip side, staying cool and objective when the other guy is obviously not can contribute tremendously to the strength of your claim of self-defense.

Escalation

Escalation occurs when someone in the fight escalates what was a non-deadly force fight into a deadly force fight. There are two ways that escalation can affect the element of Innocence. The first is if it is you who escalates the fight. This can cause you to lose the element of Innocence and therefore lose self-defense.

The second is if the other guy escalates the fight. This can cause you to regain your Innocence if you've somehow managed to lose it.

Let's talk about the first scenario, where you escalated the fight. If your attacker open-hand slaps you, but you respond with your gun, the law sees two separate and distinct conflicts. The first conflict is considered non-deadly and the other guy was to blame for it (i.e. he was the aggressor). The second is a deadly force fight, and you were the aggressor in that fight. The courts do not like seeing what ought to have been "just" a fistfight escalate into a deadly confrontation.

Let's pretend that even though his slaps weren't deadly, you drew your gun anyway. The law permits him to now draw his own gun and shoot you in self-defense, even though he "started the whole thing." Why? Because, in the eyes of the law, there were two fights. He started a non-deadly fight, but you started a deadly fight. In this circumstance, he can still be convicted for the slap that started the first non-deadly fight, but not for your death—you're responsible for that deadly force fight.

Conversely, if you win that deadly force fight, for which you're responsible, you shouldn't be held liable for the first non-deadly fight but may well still be found guilty of killing him, because you lacked legal justification for escalating the dispute into a deadly force fight.

Regaining Innocence

What happens if you are made to look like the aggressor? Perhaps you had to defend yourself against someone, and now that person's friends are telling the police that you started it.

Even worse, imagine that you momentarily lost your mind and *were* the aggressor. There are times for all of us when we are not quite at our best. The daily pressures of life, work, and family may lead even the most amiable person to respond forcefully to insulting behavior. You snapped, shoved someone, and now you are in trouble.

As the apparent or real aggressor, you've lost the ability to claim self-defense. But does that mean you've lost that ability for the duration of that conflict, no matter what you do? Not necessarily.

Whether you made the mistake of provoking the conflict or are being made to look as if you did, there still may be a way to argue self-defense at trial. There is a way to regain your Innocence for the purposes of self-defense law. You must (1) withdraw from the fight, and (2) effectively communicate your withdrawal to the other person.

If you do those two things and the other person continues to fight, then they become the aggressor in a new conflict, and you may lawfully act in self-defense against their attack.

Naturally, conditions apply!

First, the withdrawal must be made in "good faith." You must genuinely abandon the fight. This isn't a tactical withdrawal—that is, a withdrawal intended to allow you to improve your ability to fight, such as to reload or to obtain cover, then re-engage.

Second, you need to communicate your withdrawal. For practical purposes, when people run away, they are often deemed to have constructively communicated to the other person that they are withdrawing from the fight as fast as their feet will take them. That's usually sufficient to meet the communication requirement.

That's not the best way to communicate your withdrawal, though. The best way is verbally, and loud. You want others to hear you communicate withdrawal. Hopefully, those people will later testify so that there's no question that you met this second condition. It wouldn't hurt to run away while you yell, too, so you have both explicit and constructive communication.

Here's a real danger to watch out for: *it's not just you* who can regain your Innocence. So can that other guy, the one who was the aggressor in the first fight.

Imagine you are punched, but it turns out to be a case of mistaken identity—your attacker thought you were somebody else. Realizing their mistake, your attacker backs off. You, being understandably angry, decide to return the attacker's favor and give them a punch of your own.

What's happened? By backing off, the original attacker has regained his Innocence, and now you are the aggressor in a second fight. In that second fight, the guy that punched you first can claim self-defense, but you cannot.

Now, there is an important potential catch in many states. Some jurisdictions distinguish between an *initial aggressor* in a fight and a *provoker* of a fight.

I know what you're thinking: aren't the aggressor and the provoker the same thing? Don't they both mean the person who started the fight?

In many states, that is exactly correct. In those states, no distinction is drawn between an aggressor and a provoker: either can regain their innocence by withdrawing from the fight and communicating their withdrawal.

But some states do draw a distinction between an aggressor and a provoker. The meaning of aggressor remains the same, and an aggressor can still regain innocence, but a provoker is treated differently.

So what's a provoker mean in those states, and how is a provoker treated differently? In those states that draw this distinction, a provoker is someone who provokes the other person to be the first to act, with the intent of using that other person's force as an excuse to justify their own response.

We've all seen this in movies, if not in real life: some tough guy goads another person into being the first to throw a punch (or go for their gun, in Westerns), so that the tough guy now has an apparent legal justification to use force against that other person.

In states that distinguish between the initial aggressor and the provoker, the initial aggressor is allowed to regain their Innocence by withdrawal and communication.

The provoker, however, is not. The provoker owns that fight, period.

Escalation

Earlier, we discussed what happens to the element of Innocence if you escalate a non-deadly fight to a deadly force fight. Now let's consider what can happen if the other person escalates the fight.

If you start a non-deadly force fight and the other person responds with the same amount of force, then they're acting in lawful self-defense. You, as the unlawful aggressor, cannot claim self-defense, but the other person can.

But if they respond to your non-deadly force with a deadly force response, in the eyes of the law they started a second fight in. They are the aggressor in that second fight, and you are innocent. Now you can respond to their deadly force counterattack with legal defensive action.

This principle is well described in the authoritative legal treatise, *Criminal Law*, by W. LaFave and A. Scott:

> It is generally said that one who is the aggressor in an encounter with another — i.e., one who brings about the difficulty with the other — may not avail himself of the defense of self-defense. Ordinarily, this is certainly a correct statement, since the aggressor's victim, defending himself against the aggressor, is using lawful, not unlawful, force; and the force defended against must be unlawful force, for self-defense. Nevertheless, there are two situations where an aggressor may justifiably defend himself. (1) A

non-deadly aggressor (i.e., one who begins an encounter, using only his fists or some non-deadly weapon) who is met with deadly force in defense may justifiably defend himself against the deadly attack. This is so because the aggressor's victim, by using deadly force against non-deadly aggression, uses unlawful force.

Criminal Law, 2d Ed. (1986)

A recent California appellate case made essentially the same point:

California

If you decide that the defendant started the fight using non-deadly force and the opponent responded with such sudden and deadly force that the defendant could not withdraw from the fight, then the defendant had the right to defend himself with deadly force and was not required to stop fighting.

People v. Carillo, 2011 Cal. App. Unpub. LEXIS 5182 (CA Ct. App. 2011)

This approach can also be found in Kentucky, which denies self-defense to aggressors and then provides exceptions to this denial. It reads in relevant part:

Kentucky

Revised Statute §503.060

Notwithstanding the provisions of [Kentucky self-defense law], the use of physical force by a defendant upon another person is not justifiable when:

. . .

(3) The defendant was the initial aggressor, except that his use of physical force upon the other person under this circumstance is justifiable when:

    (a) His initial physical force was non-deadly and the force returned by the other is such that he believes himself to be in imminent danger of death or serious physical injury; . . .

Wrap-Up

The first element of the law of self-defense is Innocence. Legitimate self-defense is available only if you are an innocent party to the confrontation. If you initiate or sustain a confrontation, your actions cannot be justified as self-defense.

You may accurately see yourself as someone unlikely to start, continue, or escalate a confrontation. Even so, fights often begin at the low end of the force continuum and escalate. Actions or language on your part that initially seemed innocuous may later be portrayed as provoking the confrontation. Also, there may be few if any witnesses to the encounter, or the witnesses may be hostile to you.

In a few jurisdictions, words alone may be sufficient to qualify you as an aggressor. In the majority of states, though, some overt physical action must also have occurred.

In cases of mutual combat, the blows of you and your "attacker" do not cancel each other out. Instead, both of you are co-aggressors, and both lose the right to claim self-defense.

Merely being in a fight does not constitute mutual combat, however. There must be a preexisting agreement, explicit or implicit, for the parties to fight. Again, be careful. Perceptions and witnesses may not be in your favor.

Similarly, being the first to use or threaten force does not necessarily make you the aggressor, if doing so was necessary to defend yourself against an imminent attack. There is, however, a strong tendency among law enforcement and the courts to perceive striking a first blow as indicative of aggressor behavior, short of any evidence to the contrary. A compelling narrative will be needed to overcome this perception.

If you do start a fight, there are two ways you may regain your innocence:

First, withdraw from the fight and effectively communicate your withdrawal from the fight. All states allow for this if you are the initial aggressor. Many also allow this for a provoker, a person who provokes another to be the first to threaten or use force. Some states, however, deny provokers the ability to regain their Innocence by withdrawal and communication.

Keep in mind: it's not just you who can regain your Innocence—so can your attacker. If they do, and you pursue, now you're the aggressor in a second fight.

Second, the other person responds to your non-deadly force with deadly force. You are still the aggressor for the first non-deadly force fight, but they have become the aggressor for the second deadly force fight.

In short, if the criminal justice system perceives you as the bad guy, it will treat you as the bad guy, suitable for, and legally vulnerable, to successful prosecution. Any suggestion that you were wearing the "black hat" in the conflict enormously increases the likelihood you will be vigorously pursued by the criminal justice system.

Fortunately, the converse is also true. To the extent your actions appear lawful, you will appear difficult to prosecute, and the system is less likely to pursue you. The prosecutor's "story of guilt" will be substantially more difficult to craft and far less compelling.

Bottom line, it pays to keep your nose clean, especially if you're really explicit and obvious about it. Play the role of the innocent, live the role of the innocent, and you'll receive enormous dividends should you ever have to argue self-defense and are very much in need of that element of Innocence.

Chapter 3

Element 2: Imminence

The second fundamental element of the law of self-defense is Imminence. An excellent legal definition of the word is found in Black's Law Dictionary:

> Immediate danger, such as must be instantly met, such as cannot be guarded against by calling for the assistance of others or the protection of the law . . . such an appearance of threatened and impending injury as would put a reasonable and prudent man to his instant defense.
>
> *Black's Law Dictionary*, 5th Edition (1979)

In other words, if an attack is imminent, it is about to occur *right now*. So, where might you get into legal trouble with imminence? When you use force either too early or too late (or can be made to look as if you did).

If an attack is too far in the future, then you are not allowed to respond with violence. Someone who threatens to go home, get a gun, come back, and kill you does not represent imminent danger. In such circumstances, you must do something other than fight, like leave the area and call the cops.

If force has already been used against you, but ended—you've been punched, but the attacker has now fled—then that attack is in the past and no longer imminent. The law does not permit you to retaliate or hand out your own justice. That's what the police and the courts are for.

Of course, if a second incoming blow is imminent, you may protect yourself from that ongoing attack. Obviously, then, it is important to accurately judge when a threat has become imminent.

The AOJ Triad

A great tool to evaluate imminence in real-time is called the AOJ Triad. It's also good for explaining to others what happened in a way that clearly shows imminence. I first learned of the AOJ Triad as a student in Massad

Ayoob's[2] LFI-1 course (now MAG-40) way back in 1996, and have yet to find something better suited to the purpose. The AOJ stands for *ability, opportunity*, and *jeopardy*. Let's take a look at each of those in turn.

Ability

This first leg of the AOJ Triad is the component of ability, and addresses the question, "Is my attacker able to hurt me?" Almost anyone, of course, can exert some degree of force upon you.

For our purposes, then, we can just about always assume that the attacker has some ability to cause at

---

[2] By the way, I cannot let a mention of Mas' name pass without saying that virtually everyone who teaches self-defense law stands on his shoulders. It was his LFI-1 course that first led me to specialize in self-defense law. Nothing I've done since on the subject would have happened otherwise.

As I write this, we are fortunate that Mas is still teaching, and hopefully will for many decades to come. But nobody works forever. If you haven't taken the opportunity to attend one of Mas' classes, I urge you to do so post haste, at www.massadayoobgroup.com. Students who have attended both Mas' classes and my own seminars tell me they're very complementary—Mas' from the perspective of a career in law enforcement and my own from the perspective of a criminal attorney.

least a small degree of harm. The only real question is how much harm.

Opportunity

This second leg of the AOJ Triad, opportunity, addresses the question "Can their attack get to me?"

If your attacker has a gun, unless you're behind a bulletproof wall, they can use it against you. So opportunity is rarely a question when the bad guy is armed with a firearm. But what about an impact weapon—such as a knife, a club, or fists? Then your attacker will only have opportunity if there are no obstacles barring their way and they are close enough in distance to you.

Obstacles
Obstacles are barriers between you and the aggressor that get in the way of their ability to harm you. Such barriers may not be initially present, but if you can do so with complete safety placing them between you and your attacker is almost certainly a good move.

Imagine, for example, that you are in a parking lot and someone threatens you with a knife. If you can, with complete safety, position yourself so that there's a car between yourself and the attacker, that obstacle can strip them of opportunity. They can't bring that knife to bear against you unless they first overcome that obstacle. (I suppose they can throw the knife at you, but then it's your knife.)

Of course, if the attacker chases you around the car and manages to catch up, the situation has changed again. He now has opportunity as well as ability, and assuming there is jeopardy (which we will discuss in a moment), then an imminent threat exists.

Why is it almost always a good move to try to get an obstacle between you and the attacker? For several reasons.

First, none of us should be eager to get into a deadly-force fight. Just because we're the good guys doesn't mean we're going to win. What's at stake is your life. Don't put it in jeopardy unless it's truly necessary.

Second, if you have the option to remove opportunity and you choose not to do so, how might a prosecutor characterize that choice? After all, you had the option to not fight (by placing an obstacle between you and the person), and, instead, you chose to fight.

That can be made to look a lot like mutual combat. And if the jury believes it was mutual combat, you lose on the element of Innocence, as discussed in the last chapter, and there goes your claim of self-defense.

Distance

Just like with obstacles, if your attacker has a gun, then distance isn't usually helpful because firearms throw hot pieces of lead over long distances very quickly. Again, distance tends to be an issue only in the context of impact weapons, so let's consider those.

Clearly, if someone is standing beside you armed with a knife, they have the opportunity to stab you with that knife. Just as clearly, someone with a knife 100 yards away is too far away to hurt you with (unless they throw it, in which case it is now your knife).

The question, then, is at what distance between "standing next to you" and "100 yards away" does a person with an impact weapon become an imminent threat? Five feet? Or is 10 feet close enough? Fifteen feet?

Dennis Tueller, a Salt Lake City police officer and firearms instructor (since retired), asked just this question. Uniformed officers are routinely faced with impact weapon-bearing suspects (remember, fists are impact weapons). So it's natural for Tueller to wonder how far away a suspect must be for officers to have "enough" time to defend themselves against the suspect should the suspect charge at them with that impact weapon.

To answer his question, Tueller ran a bunch of empirical studies, which is just a fancy way of saying he put a bunch of students through an exercise that would later be known as the Tueller Drill.

Tueller learned that most officers could draw a service pistol from a holster and engage a threat with center-mass hits within 1.5 seconds. So the question then becomes, how much distance can a bad guy cross in 1.5 seconds?

Timing a great many students running from a standing start, Tueller learned that someone could cross about 21 feet at speed in about 1.5 seconds. So, 21 feet became the "Tueller distance," or the maximum distance from a police officer a person can be and still be capable of striking the officer before the officer can present their pistol and shoot them in self-defense.

The Tueller Drill is often referred to as the "21 foot rule," or the "7 yard rule." This really obscures the real take-home message of the Tueller Drill. The value is not some particular distance. What matters is your "Tueller distance." People's draw speeds vary. Your Tueller distance will be greater or less than 21 feet depending on your ability to get you gun unholstered and pointed center-mass.

The real lesson of the Tueller Drill is that someone armed with an impact weapon has the opportunity to use it at a far greater distance than most think—and certainly much greater distances than a juror might have otherwise thought. If you imagine the length of typical American parking space and add another three paces, you'll be right about at 21 feet.

If you shoot someone 15 feet away, a prosecutor might well try to convince the jury that 15 feet is too far for the person you shot to have had the opportunity to use the knife against you, and therefore too far for them to have been an imminent threat. Because they were not yet an imminent threat, the prosecutor will argue, the jury should deny your claim of self-defense.

If you know the Tueller Drill, however, you know that 15 feet is more than close enough for an attacker with an impact weapon to have the opportunity to bring that weapon to bear. And because you know the Tueller Drill, and you used that knowledge to make decisions in that critical moment, you have the opportunity to tell the jury about the Tueller Drill. Now the jury understands that the prosecutor's argument is false, and that story about the attacker being "too far away" gets cut off at the knees.

Defensive Display

Of course, real life is not as binary as the Tueller Drill might suggest. In the real world, we don't just sit back and watch a guy approach from 40 feet away with a raised machete, patiently twiddling our thumbs until he gets to 21 feet, then suddenly whip out our gun and shoot him. We will want to take incremental steps to defend ourselves.

Most defensive uses of a gun do not result in a shot being fired. Merely presenting the gun often solves the problem. (Of course, you can't count on this happening, so you must be prepared to shoot under the appropriate circumstances.)

Unfortunately, displaying a gun unnecessarily constitutes the serious felony offense of aggravated assault with a firearm, good for 10 or 20 years in prison, absent justified self-defense.

In some cases, a defensive display of a firearm is clearly justifiable—someone a mere six feet away who is threatening you with a knife clearly has the opportunity to hurt you. Shooting them under those circumstances might well be appropriate, and any time shooting would be permitted, showing the firearm would also be permitted.

On the other hand, if that same person with a knife is 40 feet away, shooting him is probably not justified. Yet, if firing is not justified, can you at least display your gun? Can the gun be displayed, if not fired, in situations where opportunity has not yet been reached?

States deal with the matter of defensive display in massively different ways. The cases are also extraordinarily fact-sensitive, meaning that very small changes in the facts lead to big changes in legal outcomes.

On one extreme we have states like Montana, where defensive display is explicitly permitted by statute:

Montana

> *§45-3-111. Openly carrying weapon -- display -- exemption.*
>
> (2) If a person reasonably believes that the person or another person is threatened with bodily harm, the person may warn or threaten the use of force, including deadly force, against the aggressor, including drawing or presenting a weapon.

On the other extreme we have Massachusetts, where you may only display a gun—even by just holding open your jacket to show the holstered pistol—if the circumstances justify firing it:

Massachusetts

> "Permitting the threatening of deadly force without holding the user responsible as having

actually used deadly force [would] provide a safe harbor to encourage the escalation of violence."

Commonwealth v. Cataldo, 668 N.E.2d 762 (MA Supreme Court 1996)

The large majority of states fall in between those two extremes. All states, though, are concerned about making laws that encourage escalation from what should be a non-deadly-force fight into a gunfight.

The worry for us is that if we face a real threat and defensively display our gun, will the authorities decide that the defensive display was inappropriate, and therefore unlawful?

If they decide the display was unlawful, the legal consequences can be severe. Displaying a gun in order to make another person fear death or grave bodily harm constitutes aggravated assault with a firearm, and can result in 10 or 20 years in prison. Yet that's exactly what we are doing when we display our gun defensively. We make an attacker fear what we can do to them with the handgun in an effort to deter an expected attack.

So how do we know when the authorities will decide drawing our gun was appropriate and unlikely to lead to prosecution, as opposed to when they will find it inappropriate and subject to prosecution?

As already noted, if firing it would have been OK, then the display is OK. But what about circumstances where it would not have been appropriate to shoot? When is display OK in those situations?

Unfortunately, there's no way to know for certain which defensive displays will meet with official approval and which will not. After all, the justice system is a creature with humans making the decisions, and those humans have their own interests that may or may not line up with your best interests. There's always going to be at least some risk of prosecution for a defensive display. As a result, no defensive display should even be considered if there exists any safe alternative.

Nevertheless, there are some scenarios that are much more likely to be seen as an appropriate defensive display than others. So let's discuss two model scenarios.

In both of these model scenarios, you reasonably perceive a threat. At the moment, the threat is sufficiently far away that the attacker does not yet have opportunity. But they mean business, and if nothing is done to deter them, they will inevitably get close enough to be an imminent threat.

Pretend a guy has a machete raised over his head. He is looking directly at you, calling you out by name, screaming he is going to kill you. He is deliberately closing in on you, and if nothing is done, he will inevitably attack you with deadly force.

In that kind of scenario I believe you have a very compelling argument why defensive display was justified, even before the threat became imminent.

Indeed, you can argue that pulling your gun was in your attacker's best interest. It delayed the time when you would need to use the gun. If you un-holster the gun in advance of needing it, you cut down the 1.5 seconds needed to shoot to far less, so you can afford to wait longer than if you'd kept the gun concealed.

Now let's adjust the scenario just described a little bit. Your attacker is still obviously focused on you. He is still too far away to be an imminent threat, but he is deliberately closing the distance.

One thing is different from the previous scenario, though: he lacks a machete. There is no evidence that the guy is going to use deadly force against you. There's no apparent weapon, no great disparity in size or strength, etc.

In that case, in most states you can't legally display your gun, which constitutes deadly force if used, even after he's close enough to be an imminent threat because he still isn't using or threatening deadly force.

It is in this latter scenario that prosecutors most often decide your actions were unjustified and criminal. You just made yourself very vulnerable to successful prosecution.

So, what's the answer? Obviously, you don't just want to sit there and "take it," even if the threat is "merely" non-deadly. You want to protect yourself. You have the right not to be harmed, even slightly. The answer is pretty simple: have an effective non-deadly means of self-defense in addition to your deadly means of self-defense. We'll talk more about a non-deadly means of self-defense in greater detail later in this book.

Jeopardy

Even assuming we have spotted (and can articulate) ability and opportunity, a threat is not imminent unless there is also jeopardy.

Jeopardy exists when a person with ability and opportunity conducts themselves in such a way that it reasonably appears they intend to use them against an innocent person (e.g., you).

A classic example of ability and opportunity but not jeopardy is an armed security guard at a bank. While you're waiting for a teller, the bank guard is only feet away, carrying a loaded sidearm. Clearly, he's able to hurt you. Just as clearly, there's an opportunity for him to do so. But absent the third element of reasonably apparent jeopardy, you can't shoot him because absent jeopardy he's not an imminent threat. The "J" is missing from "AOJ."

What if that armed person was not a guard, though, but a bank robber? He's the same distance and has the same gun. But unlike the guard, his conduct—"Everyone get down!" and firing the shotgun into the ceiling—is clearly a threat to use that ability and opportunity against an innocent person.

Jeopardy doesn't have to be announced. The guy doesn't have to say, "Give me all your money, or I'll kill you!" It also covers implicit threats, like someone following you through a dark parking garage with a knife held up menacingly.

The jeopardy element is probably the hardest one to be confident about. Sometimes the situation is clear. The guy is spraying bullets everywhere. But what about more ambiguous situations? What if a young man gives you a "bad feeling," but there's no weapon in sight? Telling the police "You just had to be there" is not going to cut it.

Fortunately, there are things you can do to clarify the situation. If possible, take actions that force the person to act in one way if they are a threat, but in another way if they're not.

Here's a good example. You see a menacing person approaching on your side of the street, so you cross to the other side to avoid them. He crosses too and continues to close. That's a fact—evidence!—that you share with police later to corroborate the reasonableness of your fear. Similarly, in a parking garage you can put a vehicle between you and the person. If they follow you around it, that's a good indication you're in jeopardy.

Another great way is to shout at them. "Stay back!," "Don't come closer!," "You're scaring me!," "Stop following me!," "Don't make me defend myself!," "What do you want?!," or even simply "Help! Police!"

If they still go after you after all that, there's no question that they represent jeopardy. If you were wrong about them being a threat and you unnecessarily scare away an innocent person, you may be a little embarrassed about your misinterpretation, but I'd rather be embarrassed than kill an innocent person (or be killed by an unchallenged aggressor).

The AOJ Triad is not a formal legal doctrine. But it is a useful tool to help you both identify an imminent threat in real-time and articulate to others a compelling, evidence-based narrative of a reasonably perceived imminent threat.

EXAMPLE CASE: *State v. Berriel*, 262 P.3d 1212 (UT Ct. App. 2011)

Darren Berriel's friend, Rachel, had recently told him that her boyfriend, Luis, was abusive. One day, while in the car with his friends, Berriel got an hysterical phone call from Rachel, screaming and crying that Luis was beating her. Berriel immediately turned the car around and raced to Rachel and Luis' house, only to find no one was home. Obviously still worried, Berriel decided to wait there until they returned.

It turns out Luis and Rachel had gone to pick up Rachel's younger brother, a trip of 15 to 20 minutes. When they arrived back home, there was no indication of an ongoing argument, nor did anyone appear upset.

Berriel immediately ran at Luis with a knife, and a brief fight ensued, all while Rachel was between 15 feet and 15 yards away. It ended when Berriel cut Luis, requiring stitches on his left forearm. Berriel was arrested and charged with aggravated assault.

At trial Berriel argued that his actions were justified, because he was defending both himself and Rachel. He asked the trial judge to instruct the jury about both self-defense and defense of others.

The judge agreed on self-defense, but refused to give the defense of others instruction. Berriel was convicted of third degree aggravated assault and weapons charges.

On appeal, Berriel argued that the trial judge should have given a defense of others instruction. There are three problems with this. First, the 15-minute time lapse between the phone call and when he finally saw Luis was sufficient time for an argument between Luis and Rachel to end. Second, Luis was not threatening, touching, or even approaching Rachel menacingly when they got home. Finally, during the encounter, Rachel was between 15 feet and 15 yards away, and out of the path of the fight.

While Berriel had evidence that Luis was violent to Rachel in the very recent past, by the time the fight started, Luis was not an imminent threat to Rachel. The appellate court emphasized that "it is the imminence of harm to another that is central to the legal justification of violence to prevent it; otherwise, this humane law of justification could be extended to countenance retribution or vigilantism." As a result, the three-judge appellate court, in a two-to-one decision, affirmed Berriel's felony conviction.

What is particularly interesting about Berriel's case, though, is the starkly different view of the third judge. First he noted that the relevant Utah statute gives the jury the responsibility to decide imminence, not the judge. Second, the statute includes patterns of abuse or violence in the relationship as a factor to consider. Finally, Utah law gives a low threshold, namely "if there is any reasonable basis on the evidence to justify it."

The passengers in Berriel's car had testified to the phone call, including overhearing Rachel crying and screaming. Clearly, there was imminent danger at the moment of the call. The question, then, is whether such a belief continued to be reasonable during the time that elapsed between the phone call and the fight. In the dissenting judge's view, "once Berriel had a reasonable basis to believe that Rachel was in imminent danger ... his actions in her defense were potentially justifiable...[until] Berriel had reason to believe that the danger to Rachel had passed."

The rapidity of events once Berriel encountered Luis may have "deprived Berriel of any meaningful opportunity to revise his assessment of the ongoing danger to Rachel.... and was therefore entitled to act in the continued belief that Rachel remained in danger."

On this basis, the dissenting judge believed that the trial court denied Berriel a fair trial. Unfortunately for Berriel, the majority decision decided his fate against him.

Wrap-Up

The second fundamental element of the Law of Self Defense is Imminence.

An imminent threat is one about to happen right now. Force used too soon or too late is not lawful. A threat of future harm is not an imminent threat against which defensive force can be used. Using force against another after the threat has passed is retaliation, not self-defense.

If a prosecutor successfully attacks your claim of self-defense on the principle of Imminence, your legal defense could suffer terminal damage. It is, therefore, essential to have a robust narrative that shows the imminent nature of the threat you faced.

A very useful tool to understand imminence is the AOJ Triad. The AOJ Triad stands for Ability, Opportunity, and Jeopardy, and is very helpful in two ways.

First, you can use it to evaluate whether a threat is imminent in real-time, as you are facing the threat, so you know whether you are lawfully permitted to use force in self-defense.

Second, it helps you to articulate, in a compelling and evidence-based way, why your perception of an imminent threat was a reasonable perception.

Almost everyone possesses some ability to cause harm, so ability is almost always present to some degree.

Whether your attacker has the opportunity to bring that ability to bear against you depends in part on the nature of the threat. If they are armed with a gun and can see you, they have the opportunity to bring the firearm to bear against you. On the other hand, if they are armed with an impact weapon, whether they have opportunity depends on obstacles and distance.

Jeopardy assesses whether your attacker's conduct indicates they intend you harm. A bank guard is able to harm you and has the opportunity, but is not causing you jeopardy. Bank robbers are.

Whether it's lawful to defensively display your deadly weapon depends on the totality of the circumstances. Some states explicitly allow for defensive display (but not the actual use) when facing a threat, even if the threat is non-deadly in nature. Others allow defensive display only when the actual use of deadly force would also have been permitted.

In the majority of states, defensive display of a firearm can be justified legally if the threat is deadly in nature. Unfortunately, many people made a defensive display of deadly force when the threat they were facing was merely non-deadly in nature. These people have made themselves extremely vulnerable to successful prosecution. The best solution for a non-deadly threat is displaying and/or using non-deadly, defensive force.

Chapter 4

Element 3: Proportionality

The element of Proportionality is like weight classes in wrestling. It wouldn't be a fair fight to ask a 100-pound person to go up against someone who weighs 200 pounds. For self-defense purposes, you can't pull your "200-pound" gun against a "100-pound" slap. Unlike wrestling, though, there are only two self-defense law "weight classes": deadly force and non-deadly force.

Deadly force means force readily capable of causing either death or serious bodily injury. Non-deadly force is all lesser degrees of force—that is, force not readily capable of causing death or serious bodily injury.

The force you use cannot be disproportionally greater than the force threatened your attacker uses. So, if your attacker is threatening or using only non-deadly force, your response must be limited to non-deadly force.

A deadly force response to a non-deadly force threat is a disproportional response. It loses you the element of Proportionality, and therefore loses you the legal justification of self-defense.

For the armed person, this means that you must make two separate decisions fast—you have to evaluate the force threatened against you so that you can determine the appropriate force to use in response. "Is the attack against me deadly or non-deadly force?" And "What force at my disposal can I lawfully use against that attack?"

If your attacker is using deadly force, you may respond with pretty much anything—once the fight is in the deadly force bucket, there are no further degrees of force. All deadly force is equivalent to all other deadly force.

But if they are using non-deadly force, I may not use my gun or other dangerous weapon. If they poke at my chest, a smashing punch to their face with brass knuckles may well be disproportionate and thus not lawful, if the blow causes serious bodily injury.

A conflict can begin at a non-deadly level and quickly escalate to deadly. This happens when your attacker's force increases or when your ability to defend yourself decreases.

If your attacker switches from bare hands to a weapon, or their huge thug friends join them mid-fight, the situation obviously crossed the threshold from non-deadly force to deadly force.

Or if you're beaten to the ground nearly senseless and the person continues to pound on you, their punches may now constitute force capable of causing you death or serious bodily injury because of your inability to defend yourself any longer.

Of course, the reverse is also true. What begins as a deadly confrontation can de-escalate. If it does, you must step down your defensive force so that it remains proportional to the attacking force.

Deadly Force

One would think that the difference between deadly and non-deadly force is self-apparent. One results in death, while the other doesn't. But in practice, things are a bit more complicated.

Legally speaking, deadly force is any force that can cause death or serious bodily injury. Serious bodily injury includes permanent disfigurement, long-term damage to a part of the body (such as a broken bone), rape, and even kidnapping.

Non-deadly force, in contrast, is any force that does not meet the definition of deadly force. It's everything else.

How do you determine whether a particular force is deadly? Well, if you end up dead, it was deadly. But that's not very helpful, so courts usually determine the deadly nature of the force based on what weapon is used.

Dangerous projectile weapons are always deemed deadly. This includes all guns, as well as bows or crossbows. Use them and you are legally on deadly force grounds.

Then there are weapons that are dangerous only within contact distance. This includes knives and clubs, for example.

Ordinary items that were not designed to be weapons can become deadly if they are used in a deadly way.

Pushing someone in the chest with the tip of a baseball bat may be offensive, but it's not likely to cause serious harm. Taking a home run swing at their head will.

Swinging the belt of a bathroom robe at someone in a whip-like fashion is non-deadly force. Using it as a garrote around their neck is deadly force.

The same items in each example, it's only the manner of their use that changed the nature of the force they inflicted.

Then, to muddy the water even more, there is the fistfight. We all know that bare hands can cause death. Human beings have been strangling each other for as long as there have been human beings.

Unfortunately (or fortunately, as the case may be), the courts consider bare hands to be non-deadly weapons by default. Police, prosecutors, judges, and juries view using a gun to prevent being punched skeptically. This is because people only very rarely die or suffer serious physical harm from a punch.

On the other hand, if an attacker uses their hands in a deadly-force manner (by wrapping them around your throat and squeezing, for example), then their hands are now being used to inflict deadly force, and justify a deadly-force response.

The courts could decide a punch is deadly, but generally will do so only if there are aggravating factors, such as the other guy being bigger or much stronger or demonstrable much better at fighting, if there are multiple attackers, or if the attacker keeps punching you after you are no longer able to defend yourself. In such cases, the blows, even though barehanded, would be far more devastating than in a "normal" fistfight.

Alternatively, courts will recognize that a punch was deadly force if the victim of the punch dies. That's not very helpful in the moment of self-defense, however.

EXAMPLE CASE: *State v. George Zimmerman*
Florida trial court 2013

One night George Zimmerman, the head of his Neighborhood Watch program, observed Trayvon Martin, a 17-year-old football player, walk aimlessly through his neighborhood in the rain. Martin fit the description of burglars that had recently plagued the neighborhood.

Zimmerman phoned the police and reported the suspicious activity. Martin, noticing Zimmerman observing him, fled from sight around a corner. Zimmerman told the police dispatcher that Martin had run, and the dispatcher asked Zimmerman where Martin was going.

Because Martin ran, Zimmerman followed him to try to regain sight of him, all while still on the phone with the dispatcher. When the dispatcher realized what

Zimmerman was doing, he told Zimmerman that he didn't need him to do that. Zimmerman responded, "OK," asked for police response, arranged for a meeting, and hung up.

Moments later Martin emerged from the shadows, verbally challenged Zimmerman, knocked him to the ground with a single punch, mounted him, and viciously beat him. Martin smashed Zimmerman's head against the sidewalk in what was described by an eyewitness as an "MMA-style pound-and-ground."

When Zimmerman screamed for help, to no avail, Martin put his hands over Zimmerman's mouth and nose, cutting off his breathing. In the struggle Zimmerman's jacket fell open, revealing his licensed pistol. Martin's hands moved to the side of Zimmerman's body near his gun, and Martin told Zimmerman that he was going to die. U

nable to escape, believing that Martin was trying to take his firearm and fearing unconsciousness and death, Zimmerman drew and fired a single, fatal shot into Martin's heart.

If Zimmerman had shot Martin while they were upright and fighting with fists, he would have violated proportionality. But after Martin knocked him to the ground, straddled his body, and beat him to near unconsciousness, Martin's barehanded attack transformed into deadly force. Zimmerman's gun became proportionate to the deadly force against him and was therefore lawful.

Despite his open-and-shut case, Zimmerman was enmeshed in a battle that played itself out as much in the limelight as in the courtroom. Prosecutors, politicians, media personalities, and lawyers behaved both unethically and illegally as they worked to condemn him for life to further their self-interests.

Luckily, Zimmerman had world-class legal representation in the defense team of Mark O'Mara and Don West, who executed a flawless defense. Zimmerman was also lucky to have had a fair jury that wanted true justice. They acquitted him after only a few hours of deliberations. Unfortunately, despite now being free, his life is forever changed and continues to be in danger of vigilante "justice."

Another great case that addresses the use of deadly force against a bare hands attack is *State v. Fish*.

EXAMPLE CASE: *State v. Fish*
213 P.3d 258 (AZ Ct. App. 2009)

In May 2004, Harold Fish was hiking alone in a national forest when he came across a stranger with unleashed dogs. As Fish waved to the man, the dogs began running down the trail toward him, barking and growling aggressively.

Fish yelled to the stranger to control his dogs but concluded that the stranger either would not or could not do so. In fear for his safety, Fish took out his Kimber 10mm pistol and fired a shot into the ground, dispersing the dogs to the sides of the trail.

Fish then noticed the stranger was running down the trail at him. Fish "yelled to the victim that he had not hurt the dogs, but the Victim continued to come at him with his eyes crossed and looking crazy and enraged, cursing at the Defendant and yelling that he was going to hurt [him]."

Fish kept his handgun lowered in front of him, clearly visible to the stranger, and yelled to "get back and leave [him] alone . . . at one point [he] yelled at the Victim to stop or he would shoot."

Fish believed that the stranger was going to kill him, and that he had nowhere to run because the dogs were at either side of the trail. The stranger continued to advance on Fish, making a "weird kind of punching thing" until he was about five feet from Fish. At that point Fish shot the stranger three times in the chest.

Fish covered the stranger with a tarp, placed his own backpack under his head, walked to a nearby highway, and flagged a passing car to call 911. Responding paramedics determined that the stranger was dead.

Fish gave statements at the scene to various law enforcement agents who responded, and he testified at the grand jury but not at the trial itself.

At the conclusion of the trial, the jury found Fish guilty of second-degree murder and sentenced him to ten years. He began serving that sentence while appealing his verdict.

Fortunately for Fish, the Arizona appellate court overturned his conviction. Fish was released from prison the following month, having served three years of his sentence. Finally, Fish was a free man.

So, after three harrowing years in prison, how did Fish shoot a single, unarmed attacker three times in the chest and still be found not guilty?

Although the judge instructed the jury on self-defense, he refused to tell the jury what acts constitutes unlawful force. This refusal, the appellate court decided, unfairly undermined Fish's sole legal defense.

Fish had wanted the judge to articulate three aspects of Arizona law.

First, that he could use deadly physical force against another person if it was necessary to prevent aggravated assault.

Second, an assault happens when someone intentionally places someone else in reasonable fear of imminent harm. Note that there need be no actual touching for an assault to occur, as long as Fish feared it.

Finally, that assault becomes aggravated if the assaulter restrains the victim.

Given this context, Fish argued that he was restrained because the aggressive dogs on either side of the trail prevented retreat. This made the attacker guilty of aggravated assault, which in turn made deadly force a justified response. The appellate court agreed, reversing the verdict.

It's sad to see the tremendous costs suffered by a law-abiding, loving father before his was victorious. The authorities investigated Fish, indicted him for murder, and convicted him at trial. He served three years in a serious prison before his appeal was successfully heard. And then he spent another two years waiting to find out if the prosecution's appeal to the Arizona Supreme Court would send him back to prison. The financial costs must have been absolutely staggering.

Non-Deadly Force

Police are trained to respond to an altercation with a variety of tools and strategies that range from harmless to deadly. Together these tools and strategies form what is called the "continuum of force." This continuum typically begins with physical presence, then verbal commands, and escalates all the way to lethal force. A police officer escalates or de-escalates along this continuum, as the situation requires.

Private citizens should do the same thing. In fact, sometimes threatening to use something as harmless as pepper spray is sufficient to stop a more violent conflict.

Carrying a gun without also carrying something less forceful is a lot like having a jackhammer as your only tool. It limits your options and creates a genuine risk that you may go to the gun—your only defensive tool—when a gun is not legally allowed.

The force continuum does not necessarily require you to take each individual step up and down that continuum in sequence. If you start with a commanding voice to "Stop!" and your attacker pulls out a knife, you don't have to try to use pepper spray before you can jump to your gun. All the continuum suggests is that your defensive force must be proportionate to the degree of the threat.

According to the Department of Justice, we are five times more likely to face a simple assault or battery (a non-deadly force threat) than we are an aggravated assault or battery (a deadly force threat). And this statistic is conservative. The number is probably far greater because many simple assaults are never reported to the police. So non-deadly, simple assaults are far more common than deadlier aggravated assaults.

A non-deadly defense, when effective, is preferable in many ways to a deadly-force defense. First, before you can use deadly force, you must fear deadly force. But non-deadly force is allowed if you fear even minimal physical contact, a far lower standard, and one easier to both meet and prove.

So even when you are legally allowed to use, say, a gun, if you can, consistent with safety, use non-deadly-force instead, the results will be better for everyone— assuming, of course, that making use of the non-deadly option does not increase your jeopardy.

Perhaps the most common choice is pepper spray. When first brought to market, pepper spray was always seen as a non-deadly weapon. Their rapid adoption by police was specifically to provide a less dangerous option than a nightstick or flashlight.

Never one to pass up an opportunity, criminals are increasingly using pepper spray to committing crimes.

Prosecutors naturally want to charge these criminals with as serious an offense as the facts support. So they have pushed the argument that pepper spray can be a dangerous weapon, and not merely non-deadly force. The idea is that the discomfort, pain, and incapacity caused by pepper spray constitute "serious bodily harm" or "loss of function."

So, if a robber uses pepper spray in, say, a robbery, the charge becomes armed robbery, with a much more serious sentence than simple robbery. If pepper spray is used to commit an assault, the charge becomes aggravated assault, just as if a gun had been used.

You can see the problem, though. Now if you or I use pepper spray to defend ourselves, we could be treated as if we'd used a deadly weapon rather than a non-deadly weapon, and potentially face a charge of aggravated assault charges, rather than just simple assault. The following is a recent example of the evolving status of pepper spray.

EXAMPLE CASE: *State v. Ovechka*
975 A.2d 1 (2009)

Ovechka, the defendant, had a long, simmering dispute with his neighbor, a Bridgeport police officer. The dispute culminated in the summer of 2003 when Ovechka sprayed his neighbor with pepper spray, resulting in transient conjunctivitis (literally, reddening and inflammation of the eyes) and dermatitis (literally, reddening and inflammation of the skin).

Ovechka was charged with, and convicted of, assault in the second degree. Second-degree assault in Connecticut is aggravated and must involve a "dangerous instrument."

The defendant appealed, saying the state didn't prove pepper spray was a dangerous weapon. The appellate court agreed, and reversed the second-degree charge.

The prosecution then appealed, arguing that the evidence didn't prove pepper spray wasn't dangerous. In fact, it was just the opposite. The victim was blinded, and had burns on his face, neck, and chest that remained painful for several days.

The Connecticut Supreme Court ultimately supported the guilty second-degree assault verdict. In the Court's lengthy explanation, they noted that the majority of jurisdictions have recently decided mace or pepper spray is a dangerous or deadly weapon capable of inflicting great bodily harm.

The decision was a closely divided one: four to three. Those opposed were concerned that their ruling would have bad, unintended consequences. In particular, they worried people would stop using pepper spray in legitimate defense. This point is quite pertinent. After all, we are considering what form of non-deadly force is best right now and taking into account this very case.

The majority of justices respond to this concern by noting that their ruling does not always mean the courts should consider pepper spray dangerous. Rather, it means pepper spray won't always be considered non-deadly, and permits the jury to decide if it was dangerous in each case.

Today the majority of states consider pepper spray to be at least potentially dangerous and capable of causing "serious bodily harm," even if only temporarily. Most states, though, only categorize it this way when the user is committing a crime, like bank robbery, rather than in purported self-defense. Still, it cannot now be said that pepper spray is never a dangerous weapon.

Even with all the downsides I just listed, I continue to carry pepper spray. I do so, though, with the full knowledge that I may face aggravated assault charges if I use it. I also know I can counter this by saying that, at the proper time, I used the spray as an alternative to deadlier means, aka my handgun.

Duration of Force

Just as using deadly force against a non-deadly attack breaks the element of Proportionality, how long you apply that force can also violate the element of Proportionality.

Let's say you are in the most egregious of circumstances – a psychopathic killer is shooting at you, intent on your demise. You are in a corner and have no choice but to shoot back. Your first shot hits the gunman square in the chest. He drops his gun and falls face-first to the floor, either unconscious or dead. You walk up to him, but he is unresponsive. You nudge him with your foot, and he doesn't react.

Were this a movie, Bruce Willis would deliver an "anchoring" shot to the bad guy's cranium just to be prudent. But real life isn't a movie.

Despite all the adrenaline in your system and fear that may still be lingering, you cannot "shoot him one more time just to be safe." This would break the duration of force rule. If you know that he is no longer capable of further harm, you must stop using defensive force.

People get into trouble with this when there is a pause in the fight, and two things occur.

First, he threat is neutralized.

Second, a reasonable defender would see that the threat is neutralized.

Then, the defendant chooses to use force again. A good example of this violation of the duration principle occurred in the 2013 shooting of teenager Jordan Davis by Michael Dunn.

EXAMPLE CASE: *State v. Dunn*
Florida trial court 2014

Michael Dunn was visiting Jacksonville, Florida, for his son's wedding. The wedding now over, Dunn and his fiancée stopped at a local convenience store to purchase some wine and chips for the evening. But while his fiancée was in the store, remarkable events unfolded outside, just a few feet away.

Jordan Davis, a teenager, and four friends of similar age, were driving around in a red SUV to "meet girls." They stopped at the same convenience store and parked in the spot immediately to Dunn's left.

The SUV was playing rap music very, very loud. Dunn would testify that he asked the teenagers to turn down the music. According to Dunn, Jordan Davis pointed a shotgun-like object at him and threatened to kill him.

Dunn retrieved his 9mm Taurus pistol from his glove compartment and fired at the SUV.

There were no cameras on the exterior of the convenience store, so there is no video of the shooting. There was, though, a video inside the convenience store that recorded audio, so we can hear the shots as they were fired. In combination with CSI tactics, we know which series of shots had which impact on the SUV and on the passengers inside the SUV.

It's clear by the recording there were three distinct sets of shots fired, with the first two sets very close together. The first burst of three rounds struck the rear passenger door, mortally striking Davis. The SUV driver reversed out of the parking space as Dunn fired a second burst of four rounds. These penetrated only the exterior half of the car door.

At this point the recording clearly has a full six-second pause before more gunshots are heard. During these six seconds, the SUV driver pulled out of the spot and raced away as Dunn got out of his car, stepped out into the parking lot, took a knee, and fired three more rounds at the departing SUV. Two of these rounds struck the rear bumper. The fourth traversed the SUV at head height. It was a miracle that this round struck none of the teenagers. As the SUV raced away, Dunn's fiancée exited the convenience store and they fled the scene.

The boys quickly realized that Jordan Davis was badly hurt and immediately drove back to the convenience store to call 911 for help. Tragically, Davis was beyond saving.

The police found Dunn (an interesting story in its own right) and charged him with numerous crimes, including both murder and three counts of attempted murder. Dunn would raise the legal defense of self-defense.

The trial was held, and the jury was put in deliberations. A few hours later, they returned with their verdict.

The first three rounds fired were the basis of the murder charge, because those were the rounds that killed Jordan Davis. The last three rounds were the basis of the three counts of attempted murder.

On the charge of murder, the jury was hung—that is, they could not come to a unanimous verdict. At least one juror still had a reasonable doubt that the first three rounds fired could have been lawful self-defense.

On the three charges of attempted murder, though, Dunn was declared guilty. So every single juror didn't even have a reasonable doubt that Dunn's last three shots could have been self-defense. Dunn was sentenced to life in prison ... plus 90 years.

What was the difference between the first and the last three rounds? The last three came after that lengthy six-second pause during which time the SUV tore out of the parking lot as fast possible. That makes the last three rounds excessive, unlawful, and not justifiable as self-defense.

While it is important to ensure your safety, and I wouldn't hesitate to continue shooting until my deadly force attacker was no longer an imminent deadly threat, the more bullet holes you put in your attacker the more likely it will be seen as a duration-of-force problem.

No one looks at a body with 30 bullet holes or 45 knife slashes and says, "Classic case of self-defense."

If you did need to use that much force, you will also need a compelling explanation for it in your self-defense narrative that doesn't include any gaps in time where the threat disappeared.

Wrap-Up

The third fundamental element of the law of self-defense is Proportionality. The degree of force you use to defend yourself must be proportionate to the degree of force used by your attacker(s). Any degree beyond that is excessive and unlawful.

Force used in self-defense may be excessive in intensity or excessive in duration. Excessive intensity occurs when you counter a non-deadly force threat with a deadly force defense. Excessive duration happens when you continue to use force after the threat is neutralized, and a reasonable person would have perceived the threat to be neutralized.

Deadly force includes force likely to cause death or serious bodily injury. Serious bodily injury includes a debilitating injury, the loss of function of a part of the body, rape, and kidnapping. Deadly attacks may be defended against with either deadly force or non-deadly force.

Non-deadly force is any physical force that doesn't meet the "death or serious bodily harm" threshold. Any unwanted touching, however slight, is sufficient to justify a proportional use of defensive non-deadly force.

A conflict that starts as non-deadly can easily transition to a deadly force encounter, and vice versa. The armed citizen must be able to adjust their response to changing circumstances. For this reason, it is prudent to arm yourself with both deadly and non-deadly weapons.

Having only a firearm as an option for self-defense leaves no good way to respond to a non-deadly attack, other than to use excessive force. This is particularly relevant given that you are far more likely to be the victim of a non-deadly attack than of a deadly attack.

Guns are always considered deadly force, but most other common objects may also become deadly even if not specifically designed for that purpose. For example, baseball bats and hammers are designed as sporting equipment and hand tools, respectively, yet they could easily cause deadly harm.

Even bare hands, usually deemed non-deadly force, can be used in a deadly fashion to, say, asphyxiate another person. Bare hands can also be deadly if the attack continues after one person is incapacitated or defenseless.

The general principle, then, is that you may resort to deadly force in self-defense when there exists such a disparity of force between you and your attacker that deadly force is necessary to stop an imminent threat of death or grave bodily harm.

Non-deadly contact weapons—such as one's bare hands —can not be used effectively until the attacker has closed the distance. Projectile weapons, such as pepper spray, can be used while the attacker remains at some distance.

Pepper spray, however, may be considered a dangerous weapon under the law, depending on the manner of its use. This raises the risk that its use could be deemed excessive force if it is used to thwart a mere non-deadly force attack.

A non-deadly defense is preferred, if effective, because the threshold for the use of non-deadly force is quite low. All you need fear is any unwanted touching. Contrast this to the threshold required for deadly defensive force, which is fear of death or serious bodily injury.

Force can also be excessive in duration. This is where, after the attacking force has stopped being a danger, you continue to use force against them. While it is vitally important to ensure your safety, do not respond with defensive force longer than is necessary to stop the attack.

Chapter 5

Element 4: Avoidance

As with all the elements of the law of self-defense, on the surface, the fourth element, Avoidance, is mostly about common sense. It makes sense to not shoot someone if you can instead get safely away and call the police. A simple enough concept, but handling it from a legal perspective can be more challenging than you might think.

These days the phrase "stand your ground" is a political lightning rod and a subject worthy of an entire book. To keep this one shorter than a phonebook, I will focus solely on the legal effects of "stand your ground" and will ignore the political dynamics.

The debate over laws requiring retreat isn't about the benefits of retreat (as noted, I urge you to always retreat from a fight, if safely possible) but about practical problems that arise by imposing a legal duty to retreat.

Duty to Retreat

In "Duty to Retreat" states, you must retreat, if safely possible, before you are permitted to use defensive force. In most of these states retreat is required only before using deadly force, but not non-deadly force. In four states, however, retreat is required before you may use even non-deadly defensive force.

No state requires unsafe retreat. You do not have to flee if doing so increases your jeopardy. You don't, for example, need to try to run across a busy freeway to escape.

The courts recognize many circumstances where safe retreat is impossible. The attack might be too sudden, for example, or the nature of the threatened force prevented retreat. If the bad guy's armed with a gun, you can't outrun a bullet. If he is in a car and you are on foot, avoidance might be difficult, to say the least.

There are other more subjective reasons that retreat may not be safely possible. Let's say you are in a state that does not require retreat when you're defending yourself with a non-deadly weapon. In such a state, as long as you are only engaging in fisticuffs, you don't need to worry about whether you could have retreated. But what if your attacker escalates to deadly force? If a safe avenue of retreat is available to you, you must now use it before you respond with deadly force.

What if during the non-deadly portion of the attack, you suffered an injury that prevented retreat? What would have been a safe avenue when you were still healthy is no longer safe now that you are injured. You are now under no duty to try to make the attempt because safe retreat is no longer possible.

The need to protect a third party can also limit your retreat options. Say, for example, that you are walking with an elderly grandfather. If there's a path of escape that's safe for you, but not safe for Grandpa, you aren't required to leave him behind.

There are also some scenarios where you almost certainly can retreat with complete safety: when you are in your car and can simply drive away from an impact-bearing aggressor, or when you are standing within an easily securable doorway. If you can easily close and lock that door to avoid the danger, not doing so is a failure to retreat.

But what if you retreat as required and your attacker pursues you? Is it enough that you've retreated once? Have you now "checked that box?"

Unfortunately, no. You must continue to fall back until it isn't safely possible to do so any longer—to "retreat to the wall." Only once your safe path out ends or becomes unsafe has your duty to retreat been satisfied.

A case out of Ohio illustrates what can happen if you retreat, but not quite far enough.

EXAMPLE CASE: *State v. Barnes*
2000 Ohio App. LEXIS 3294 (OH Ct. App. 2000)

One night Marcus Barnes and his girlfriend, Rebecca Vanaman, attended a party together. While there, Marcus came into a room to find a man named Thomas Jenior restraining another man. He intervened, and a verbal exchange ensued between him, Thomas, and a few others. Marcus, trying to avoid further conflict, walked away from the conversation and went looking for his girlfriend to leave. He couldn't find her, so he decided to go to their parked car to wait for her to come out. While there he armed himself with a knife, in fear that the confrontational men at the party would attack him.

In fact, two of the men, Christopher DeAngelis and Christopher Warren, did seek him out and attacked him at his car. Marcus killed one of his attackers with the knife and wounded the other.

At court the jury determined that although Marcus had retreated, he had not retreated far enough. He could have left the area entirely and thereby avoided the need to defend himself. The jury apparently concluded that by arming himself, he was choosing to "stand his ground." Marcus was convicted of manslaughter and felonious assault and sentenced to 15 years. He lost his appeal. The one dissenting appellate judge's point, that driving off required leaving his girlfriend behind with hostile men, did not convince the rest of the court.

Castle Doctrine

Every state with a duty to retreat has at least one exception to that duty: You do not have to retreat when you are in your home. This principle is called *the Castle Doctrine*.

This means even though you could safely escape up your stairs into your bathroom or out your back door, you are not required to do so even in a duty to retreat state; at least not from genuine intruders, most of the time.

The term Castle Doctrine derives from William Blackstone's *Commentaries on the Laws of England*, where he wrote,

"The law of England has so particular and tender a regard to the immunity of a man's house, that it stiles it his castle, and will never suffer it to be violated with impunity."

Curtilage

Every state defines what makes up your castle a little differently. Massachusetts has the most restrictive definition. It includes only the space "within the four walls of your dwelling." Place even one foot outside your front door, and you lose your Castle Doctrine privileges and once again bear a duty to retreat.

Most other states also include an area around your home known as the *curtilage* as part of your "castle." Curtilage is a loosely defined area immediately surrounding the home that is part of the normal day-to-day use of that house. It typically includes your front porch, your yard, a detached garage, and so forth, depending on the state and the manner of use of that space or structure.

Place of Business and Occupied Vehicles

More than half of the "Duty to Retreat" states have expanded the concept of the Castle Doctrine to also include one's place of business. Three states have expanded the Castle Doctrine to include your own occupied vehicle.

Exceptions to the Castle Doctrine

This being the ever-complicated legal realm, some states have made exceptions to the Castle Doctrine, which is itself an exception to the duty to retreat. So these are exceptions to the exception.

The Castle Doctrine defines locations where you do not have to retreat because you are relieved of an otherwise existing generalized legal duty to retreat. Exceptions to the Castle Doctrine make you once again have to retreat, even within a "castle" area, by re-imposing that generalized legal duty to retreat.

One of these exceptions to the Castle Doctrine applies if you don't have a right to be in your home. How can that be, you might wonder?

Well, if you are in the middle of a divorce and your soon-to-be ex-wife obtains a restraining order against you, then you are no longer allowed into your former home even though your name is still on the deed.

If you show up one day and have to fight off her new boyfriend's attack, you can't use the Castle Doctrine in your defense to claim you should be relieved of an otherwise existing duty to retreat.

The Castle Doctrine also does not apply if you were the aggressor. Of course, Chapter 2, on Innocence, taught us that being the aggressor is enough on its own to strip you of your right to claim self-defense.

Let's say, though, that you started a non-deadly fight that the other guy escalated to deadly force. Even though you are not the aggressor in the second deadly force fight, having been the aggressor in the non-deadly fight may still strip you of Castle Doctrine privileges.

The Castle Doctrine is intended to relieve you from having to retreat from a fight not of your own making, it's not intended to turn a person's castle into a kind of Thunderdome.

Even if you are in your own home, and you have a right to be there, and you didn't start the fight, in some states you must still retreat if your attacker also lives there, in other words if it's also their castle. This is called the "co-habitation exception," and it can even apply to invited guests.

Fortunately, it is simple enough to convert a guest to a trespasser: order them to leave. If they do not, they're no longer guests but trespassers, and the co-habitation exception no longer applies.

Stand Your Ground

Today a large majority of states, about three-quarters of them, don't impose a generalized legal duty to retreat even when it's safe to do so. Instead, they allow innocent people, who are in a place they are allowed to be in, to defend themselves, subject only to the remaining four elements of self-defense: Innocence, Imminence, Proportionality, and Reasonableness.

States that have had this "no retreat" rule for many decades often call them "True Man" laws while those that adopted this rule more recently tend to call them "Stand Your Ground" laws. Both are essentially the same.

The media often gets the meaning of Stand Your Ground laws wrong. They say such things as "a defendant claimed Stand Your Ground, rather than self-defense."

This is legally nonsensical statement. Stand Your Ground laws merely relieve you of the element of Avoidance. You are still claiming self-defense in all other respects, and you must still qualify under the remaining four required element: Innocence, Imminence, Proportionality, and Reasonableness.

In other words, (1) If you are an innocent person attacked by an aggressor; (2) if the attack was imminent and about to happen right now; (3) if you used only proportional defensive force; and (4) if your perceptions, decisions, and actions were those of a reasonable person, then Stand Your Ground states say that you won't go to jail for the rest of your life simply because you arguably failed to take advantage of some allegedly safe avenue of retreat.

But if you fail on any of those other, still required, elements—for example, if you used disproportionate force—Stand Your Ground is irrelevant. In such a case, because you failed a still-required element of self-defense—in this example, the element of Proportionality—you were not acting in self-defense at all. Stand-Your-Ground cannot save you from such a defect in your claim of self-defense.

The greatest value of Stand Your Ground from my perspective is that it limits the power of overreaching prosecutors. Remember, the jurors and the judge were not present at the time of the attack. They didn't experience the fear and adrenaline, the literal fight for their life.

A prosecutor might show them a sketch of the scene and ask, "Why didn't the defendant just escape this way, or that way, or this third way? The defendant didn't have to kill that poor victim. The defendant could have just been the bigger person and walked away."

This whole speech is given, of course, in the guarded safety of an air-conditioned courtroom.

The defense, then, has to counter this narrative with a far more complicated story. You didn't know of that avenue of retreat because at the time, there was a truck blocking your view of it. Of course, no one took note of the truck at the time. It didn't seem important.

Or, you couldn't take advantage of that second avenue because you'd hurt your leg at work the week before and couldn't run fast enough to safely access it. Of course, the injury wasn't bad enough to go to a doctor, so there's no medical record of it.

And with respect to that third route of retreat, well, you simply didn't see it in the stress of the moment. Obviously, there can be no record of this kind of understandable oversight.

On one hand the prosecutor made up a very nice, glossy, easy-to-understand sketch of these several routes of safe escape. On the other hand, you have your own rather vague, unsupported, self-serving "excuses" why you didn't take advantage of any of them. It's not hard to see how easily this severely damages an otherwise apparently sound self-defense claim.

The adoption of a Stand Your Ground statute takes that particular "weapon" out of the prosecutor's hands. They can't destroy your right to argue self-defense just because adrenaline got in the way of seeing escape.

Be careful here, though. In some Stand Your Ground states, even though retreat isn't required, not doing so can still fail the fifth element of self-defense, Reasonableness (which we will explain further in the next chapter).

In those "soft" Stand-Your-Ground states a prosecutor can't argue that you had a duty to retreat (because you don't) but they can argue that retreat was so apparent that not doing so was unreasonable.

In effect, this is a backdoor way of attacking your claim of self-defense on the basis of your failure to retreat, through the element of Reasonableness, even when Stand-Your-Ground prevents a prosecutor from attacking the element of Avoidance directly.

There are, however, a half-dozen Stand Your Ground states that do not allow retreat to be mentioned in court at all. Here's some example statutes and case law from a few "Hard" Stand-Your-Ground states:

Mississippi

§ 97-3-15. Homicide; justifiable homicide; use of defensive force; duty to retreat.

(4) A person who is not the initial aggressor and is not engaged in unlawful activity shall have no duty to retreat before using deadly force [in self-defense] if the person is in a place where the person has a right to be, and no finder of fact shall be permitted to consider the person's failure to retreat as evidence that the person's use of force was unnecessary, excessive or unreasonable.

Texas

A person is not required to retreat before using force if he has a right to be present at that location, has not provoked the person against whom the force is used, and is not engaged in criminal activity at the time the force is used; a factfinder may not consider whether the actor failed to retreat for purposes of determining whether he reasonably believed that the use of force was necessary.

Turner v. State, 2015 Tex. App. LEXIS 8559 (TC Ct. App. 2015)

Wisconsin

> *§939.48 Self-defense and defense of others.*
> (1)(m)(ar) If an actor intentionally used force that was intended or likely to cause death or great bodily harm, the court may not consider whether the actor had an opportunity to flee or retreat before he or she used force ...

Some states place specific conditions on the ability qualify for Stand Your Ground. In Kentucky, Oklahoma, and Pennsylvania, for example, you must not have been engaged in illegal activity of any kind.

Kentucky

> [T]he evidence irrefutably established that Appellant was engaged in an unlawful activity at the time of his altercation with [the Victim]. He was concluding an illegal drug deal. Because he was engaged in an unlawful activity, Appellant was not entitled to the "no duty to retreat" instruction.
> *Jackson v. Commonwealth*, 2016 Ky. LEXIS 10 (KY Supreme Court 2016)

Oklahoma

> A person may use deadly force with no duty to retreat when he has the lawful right to be where

he is, and when he reasonably believes the use of deadly force is necessary. [However, here the defendant] was engaged in illegal activity and not entitled to benefit from the provisions of the Stand Your Ground law.

Dawkins v. State, 252 P.3d 214 (OK Ct. App. 2011)

Pennsylvania

On June 28, 2011, the legislature amended the self-defense statute to include a Stand Your Ground law. This law abolishes the common law duty to retreat for an actor who is not engaged in illegal activity, and is not in illegal possession of a firearm.

Commonwealth v. Williams, 2012 PA Super 99 (PA Superior Court 2012)

Be forewarned, though, in many such states *any* unlawful activity can undermine your Stand Your Ground privileges. For example, in some jurisdictions you can't carry concealed if you are intoxicated. A failed breathalyzer, for example, could lose you your Stand Your Ground privileges.

Wrap-Up

The fourth fundamental element of the law of self-defense is *Avoidance*.

In practical application, Avoidance refers to a legal duty to take advantage of a safe avenue of retreat before resorting to the use of force against an attacker.

Today the majority of jurisdictions do not have an explicit duty to retreat, but a sizeable minority are "Duty to Retreat" states that do require you to take advantage of any safe avenue before using force in self-defense. In "Duty to Retreat" jurisdictions your failure to retreat when it is safe to do so is fatal to your self-defense claim.

In those jurisdictions, any evidence that you did not retreat where safely possible will make you appear an attractive and vulnerable subject of arrest, indictment, prosecution, and conviction. Expect prosecutors in "Duty to Retreat" states attack this element aggressively.

Courtroom analysis, done in the absence of adrenaline and fear, is rich territory for the prosecution to craft a narrative of avoidable conflict. Overzealous prosecutorial attack using the duty to retreat has been a primary driver behind the widespread adoption of Stand Your Ground laws.

States that have Stand Your Ground laws do not have a duty to retreat, sometimes subject to certain conditions.

For example, in Kentucky you may "stand your ground" only when you are in a place you have a right to be, not engaged in unlawful activity, and not the aggressor in the conflict. If you do not meet these requirements, you once again must retreat, if safely possible, before using deadly force to defend yourself.

All "Duty to Retreat" states exclude your home under the Castle Doctrine, relieving you of the duty to retreat while in your castle, with important conditions. Some define your castle as limited to the space within the four walls of your home; others include your dwelling's curtilage, your occupied vehicle, or your place of work.

Stand Your Ground is not some odd, alternative means of arguing self-defense. It only relieves you of a legal duty to retreat before using force in self-defense. You must still qualify under every other element of self-defense: Innocence, Imminence, Proportionality, and Reasonableness.

Chapter 6

Element 5:
Reasonableness

The fifth and final fundamental element of the Law of Self Defense is *Reasonableness*.

Reasonableness can be thought of as an umbrella that covers each of the other four elements. Everything you do in self-defense—your perceptions, your decisions, and your actions—must be reasonable. As a quick recap of those other elements:

- *First Element: Innocence*: Was your belief that you were defending an innocent person, whether yourself or someone else, a reasonable belief?

- *Second Element: Imminence*: When you assessed the danger as imminent, was that a reasonable assessment?

- *Third Element: Proportionality*: Were your estimates of the degree of force threatening you, and the degree of force you used in response, reasonable?

- *Fourth Element: Avoidance*: Was your decision that there was no safe way to retreat a reasonable decision?

If you answer any of these questions in the negative, your actions were "unreasonable" and thus not lawfully justified.

But what does it mean to be reasonable, and how is a jury instructed to decide if you acted reasonably? The term "reasonable" begs a poet to wax philosophical, but that's hardly how our justice system works.

The criminal justice system, seeking to be practical, applies a two-part test to see if a defendant acted reasonably. The first test is called "objective reasonableness" and the second, "subjective reasonableness."

Objective Reasonableness

Objective reasonableness uses a notional person called "the reasonable and prudent person." A figment of the legal imagination, the reasonable and prudent person has the rather annoying tendency to do everything the right way. Let's call him Reasonable Ralph. Your actions will be judged in comparison to Reasonable Ralph. If he would do no differently, were he in your shoes, your actions were "reasonable."

So what would Reasonable Ralph do? Ralph's actions have a few standard characteristics common to all responsible adults.

Reasonable Ralph is ordinary, cautious, responsible, sober, and slow to anger. He knows the basic facts of the world, but has no great education beyond that, and possesses no particular specialized knowledge. He knows that guns are dangerous, but not the difference between "ballistics" and "terminal ballistics." He knows fire is hot, but not the exact temperature where iron melts. He knows blood loss is bad, but not how much is lethal.

Reasonable Ralph is also cautious. He looks both ways when he crosses the street, obeys the speed limit, cuts away from himself when he uses a knife, and adheres strictly to the four rules of gun safety. He does not undertake unnecessary risk, and he abides by safety guidelines.

Reasonable Ralph is responsible. He doesn't leave his car running while he runs into the store for a loaf of bread; he doesn't leave small children unattended for a "couple of minutes." And when he borrows a tool, he returns it promptly and in as good or better condition than when he received it.

Reasonable Ralph is sober. While he may drink socially, he does not do so to excess, and he always avoids public intoxication. He certainly does not drink and drive or handle dangerous equipment.

Reasonable Ralph is slow to anger. He's a "Sticks and stones may break my bones, but words will never hurt me" kind of guy. If there is any way to avoid a physical conflict, Ralph will take it, even at the cost of some personal embarrassment.

Customizing the Reasonable and Prudent Person

Reasonable Ralph, then, begins as an ideal reasonable and prudent person. Before we can apply him to any particular case, though, he needs to be "customized" to be a bit more like the defendant in that case.

If you're that defendant, Ralph needs to be given some of your particular mental and physical attributes, and be put in the situation you faced when you defended yourself.

Circumstances

In terms of the circumstances, virtually everything is taken into account. Was it a bright and clear afternoon, or a dark and stormy night? Did the conflict take place in the middle of a raging riot, or were you awakened from bed in the middle of the night by the sound of breaking glass? Was the other person quietly going on about his business, or was he repeatedly threatening you?

These and many other aspects of that fateful point in time can all be considered. So the question isn't merely WWRD—"what would Ralph do?"—but rather, WWRDITSOSC—"what would Ralph do in the same or similar circumstances?" A mouthful, for sure, but more accurate.

Characteristics

Like the circumstances, Reasonable Ralph's physical characteristics are also adjusted to match your own. Are you young and fit, or old and feeble? Did Mr. Miyagi himself train you to street fight? Do you have a handicap that would limit your ability to respond effectively to the threat? Reasonable Ralph takes on these and all other physical characteristics you had at the time of the attack.

Specialized Knowledge

As I previously mentioned, Reasonable Ralph has basic common knowledge. But can he also have any "specialized" knowledge that you possessed at the time of the encounter and that impacted your decisions? Absolutely.

Indeed, such knowledge is probably essential to your story. As such, the amount of knowledge you can give to Reasonable Ralph is huge.

You may be wondering what kind of specialized knowledge might be important to add. After all, you may know the average wingspan of an African swallow, but that probably doesn't matter.

One example of a very useful piece of specialized knowledge that may have been highly relevant to your use-of-force decision-making is something we discussed back in the chapter on Imminence: the Tueller Drill.

You will recall from the Tueller Drill that the attacker can be as far as 21 feet away and still represent an imminent threat. To someone not informed about the Tueller Drill, though, it may appear that 18-feet is far too distant. Indeed, a prosecutor might later argue precisely that to the jury.

"That poor victim," the prosecutor argues, "couldn't possibly have hurt this defendant with a knife from 18 feet away." The prosecutor paces off 18 feet from the jury box, holding a pen in place of a knife, to illustrate his point.

You watch the jurors nod in agreement. You can tell they're thinking Reasonable Ralph would not have used deadly force at that distance. You watch as the jurors reframe you as "unreasonable." The prosecutor tells the jury they must find you, the trigger-happy killer, guilty, to bring the victim "justice," and for the "protection of society."

When your lawyer gets their turn, however, the jury hears another perspective entirely. He brings in an expert witness on the Tueller Drill, like a professional firearms trainer or police trainer.

That expert explains the Tueller Drill to the jury, and its implications in your case. He says the Tueller Drill is taught to every law enforcement officer in the country. Police officers know that a suspect is an imminent threat at 18 feet, and that defensive action is objectively reasonable. If it's reasonable for police officers, it's reasonable for you, too, he explains.

After hearing that expert witness testify, the jury now possesses the specialized knowledge of the Tueller Drill. They can decide whether Reasonable Ralph would act as you had done if he knew about it too.

Knowledge of Attacker's Reputation or Past Acts

There is another type of specialized knowledge that's really useful to your case: what you knew about your attacker. Was your attacker a hothead thug with a long rap sheet? Did you know he was?

That your attacker's reputation and history might be admissible at all is an oddity of self-defense law. Generally speaking, reputation evidence is not admissible in court. At trial, the jury is supposed to make decisions based on what happened in the case before them, not unrelated acts.

Self-defense cases, though, provide exceptions to these rules. Why? Because your attacker's history can be uniquely relevant to a self-defense claim.

If you know that the person menacing you is a vicious street fighter, you might reasonably use force sooner, or use a higher degree of force, than you would have done otherwise.

Similarly, if you had previously witnessed your attacker savagely beat someone, that knowledge would almost certainly affect your take on the situation. Knowing the attacker's propensity for sudden violence likely drove your decision to respond with force when you did, and with the degree of force you used, and so the jury should account for that information when they consider your actions. Reasonable Ralph, then, will possess similar knowledge of his attacker.

Non-Prior Specialized Knowledge
What if you can't prove you knew the Tueller Drill at the time you acted in self-defense?

Then the jury will never hear about it. There will be no expert witness informing the jury of your imminent danger as proven by the Tueller Drill. Your lawyer will fumble around trying to convince the jury of the real danger you experienced without evidence to prove it.

This makes sense. If you only learned about the Tueller Drill later, then it can't have informed your decision making at the time. Reasonable Ralph would not have acted on what he didn't know. So if you want to introduce specialized knowledge to the jury, you must prove you had that knowledge at the time you acted in self-defense.

For this reason, I recommend you document your self-defense training. Underline or circle the passage on the Tueller drill in this book and put the date in the margin. Hold on to the dated receipt of your purchase. Now you possess solid documentation to prove you knew the Tueller Drill.

There are other approaches to this as well. When I took Massad Ayoob's Lethal Force Institute, Level I class about 20 years ago, all of us in the class took extensive notes. (That class is still taught today, as MAG-40.) Mas suggested that we make a copy of those notes, keep the copy in an accessible place as a reference, and place the originals in a sealed envelope, and mail them to ourselves, receipt required upon delivery.

If necessary, that USPS-dated envelope can be unsealed in court later to prove what we had learned as of that date—presumably a date earlier than the later use-of-force event.

That level of effort is required to be able to prove you possessed some particular specialized knowledge as of a certain date—but it doesn't hurt. And I can tell you that to this day I still have my envelope from LFI-I, still sealed, in a secure location.

So, as just described, the general rule is that you must be able to prove you knew any specialized knowledge before the attack if that specialized knowledge is to be presented in court as an explanation for your use-of-force decisions and actions.

There is one exception to this rule, though. This exception occurs only with the first element – innocence – and only in a limited way.

If the prosecution argues that you, not the other guy, started the fight (i.e. bring up the issue of innocence), the court will then allow you to show the jury evidence of the other guy's reputation for violence or history of violence. They'll allow it even if you did not know it at the time you acted in self-defense.

Why is this permitted? After all, this specialized knowledge could not have informed your actions if you did not possess it at the time of the use-of force event.

And that's true—it could not have informed your actions. It could, however, explain the other guy's actions.

The courts see this character evidence as meaningful to a jury trying to figure out who most likely started the fight. It also helpfully counters the prosecutor's claim that you were the aggressor.

Of course, the prosecutor is well aware that arguing about innocence opens the door to evidence of the other guy's violent history. They'd naturally rather not open that door if the guy was a massive hothead or career violent criminal.

The prosecutor may therefore make the strategic decision to pass on attacking your claim of self-defense on the issue of initial aggressor, to prevent opening that evidentiary door, and instead attack your claim of self-defense on one of the other elements, instead.

If they don't attack the element of Innocence, then it's very unlikely you will get the other guy's reputation into court unless you can show you knew of it at the time of the use-of-force event, for reasons already discussed.

Mental Characteristics

Like physical characteristics, Reasonable Ralph can also adopt your mental state at the time. Mental characteristics include normal emotions that one would expect a reasonable person to experience.

Apprehension and fear are normal if armed assailants are chasing you down a dark alley. The jury should consider whether your actions were those of a reasonable person experiencing apprehension and fear.

As famously put by the United States Supreme Court:

> "Detached reflection cannot be demanded in the presence of an uplifted knife."
> *Brown v. United States*, 256 U.S. 335 (1921)

Not all mental characteristics will be considered, though. Extreme emotions aren't admissible for the simple reason that they're not reasonable.

An easily frightened person may become terrified when someone merely points a finger at them. But such excessive fear is unreasonable and will not be considered by the jury as sufficient to justify that person's use of force. The same applies to a clinically diagnosed mental condition, such as schizophrenia. As put by a recent Texas decision:

Texas

> A "reasonable belief" is one that would be held by an ordinary and prudent person, not by a paranoid psychotic. Appellant's repeated claim that "his paranoid ideations and active psychosis" raise a "reasonable belief" that his actions were justified is supported neither by law nor common sense.
>
> *Mays v. State*, 318 S.W.3d 368 (TX Ct. App. 2010)

Similarly, Reasonable Ralph will never be drunk while acting in self-defense. The jury will not be asked to judge whether your conduct was that of a "reasonable drunk person."

This doesn't mean you you're not allowed to defend yourself after a few drinks. You have all the same rights as you had when you were sober. But you also have the same responsibilities when you defend yourself. You don't get any breaks on the element of Reasonableness just because you're voluntarily intoxicated.

If you behaved unreasonably because you were drinking, then you were unreasonable. Period. The jury will ignore your intoxication and only consider if your actions were those of a reasonable sober person. Getting drunk is your problem and not an excuse for bad behavior.

Massachusetts

> The defendant's belief cannot be deemed reasonable on the ground that, due to intoxication, he misapprehended the situation. A determination as to whether a defendant's belief concerning his exposure to danger was reasonable may not take into account his intoxication.
>
> *Commonwealth v. Barros*, 425 Mass. 572 (MA Supreme Court 1997)

Texas

> That he also claims he was drinking and unable to perceive the risk similarly does not, in light of the record, constitute evidence appellant was unable to perceive the risk created by his conduct. Voluntary intoxication is a not a defense.
>
> *Hart v. Texas*, 2011 Tex. App. LEXIS 3996 (2011)

So, where do law-abiding people run into trouble with objective reasonableness? It's the simple fact that even the best of us can have a bad day. If you allow yourself to be goaded by jerks into acting unreasonably, don't be surprised when the system compares you unfavorably to Reasonable Ralph.

Alternatively, perhaps you acted reasonably but the prosecutor makes a convincing argument that you did not. Or perhaps you acted reasonably on that particular occasion, but you have a reputation in the community for acting unreasonably at other times.

If your actions are perceived as unreasonable, then you've lost the required element of Reasonableness and your use of force against another cannot be justified as self-defense. We'll come back to the vital importance of this point when we discuss your legally-sound self-defense strategy, in the next chapter.

Subjective Reasonableness

Where objective reasonableness decides whether you did what Reasonable Ralph would have done, subjective reasonableness looks at whether you had a genuine, good faith belief that what you were doing was reasonable.

Let's pretend that you defended your life and are now a defendant at trial. Let's also say your actions were exactly what Reasonable Ralph would have done if he had been in your shoes. So objective reasonableness is not a problem.

If you didn't think you needed to use force, though, then you fail on subjective reasonableness. More accurately, if the prosecution can convince the jury that you did not have a genuine, good faith belief that the threat was imminent, deadly, and so on for each of the elements, then the jury must find your actions subjectively unreasonable.

After all, just because Reasonable Ralph would have believed force was necessary doesn't mean you did.

You might wonder how anyone could know what you were thinking. Isn't that all inside your head? Well, in an absolute sense, they can't know—but they can make reasonable inferences from your own words and conduct.

For example, you might tell others about your subjective state of mind. If a defender says that they were not really afraid, they knew they could handle that guy with no trouble, he was never really a threat to them, he just needed to be taught a lesson—those statements can be used by the prosecution to argue that you fail the requirement of subjective reasonableness. You lacked a genuine, good faith belief that your use of force was necessary for your personal safety.

More commonly, though, it is conduct rather than words that undermine subjective reasonableness. This often comes in the form of consciousness of guilt conduct, like flight from the scene for purposes other than safety, hiding from the police, or tampering with evidence.

Please don't ever flee the scene, hide from the police, or destroy evidence. If you do, the judge may tell the jury to consider such conduct as evidence that you possessed a consciousness of guilt, and give the jury a consciousness of guilt jury instruction.

Such an instruction tells the jury that not only does the prosecution believe you're guilty, your own conduct suggests that *you* think you're guilty. It's difficult to overstate how damaging this can be.

Even if you didn't do anything to suggest guilt, you still may do something that goes against the very idea of self-defense. For example, if you followed someone as they backed away during an argument it suggests that you didn't have a genuine, good faith, subjective belief that they would hurt you. A reasonable person does not pursue pain.

If it appears like you went to the fight, rather than the fight coming to you, that rarely looks like self-defense to anybody.

Again, the prosecution need only attack subjective reasonableness on any one of the four other elements— that is, that you lacked subjective reasonableness in the context of Innocence, Imminence, Proportionality, or Avoidance. If the prosecutor can do so on any one of them, they will destroy your self-defense case.

Reasonable Mistakes

What about if you *mistakenly* perceive a threat? Let's say you are being robbed at gunpoint. You manage to get out your own gun, shoot, and kill your attacker.

Then it turns out that the attacker's gun wasn't real — it was just a very realistic-looking toy. You truly believed you were facing a threat of death or grave bodily harm, but, in fact, you were not. You were hoodwinked.

Fortunately, the law does not require us to conduct ourselves perfectly, only reasonably. Mistakes are acceptable so long as they are reasonable mistakes.

If you believed the gun was real, and Reasonable Ralph would have too, then the fact that the gun was not real is simply not relevant. The law allows you to rely on that reasonable perception of a threat, and act in self-defense exactly as if the gun were real.

A good example where the law recognizes this doctrine of reasonable perception can be found in California's jury instructions:

California

> *CALJIC No. 5.51, Self-Defense—Actual Danger Not Necessary, as given:*
> Actual danger is not necessary to justify self-defense. If one is confronted by the appearance of danger which arouses in his mind, as a reasonable person, an actual belief and fear that he is about to suffer bodily injury, and if a reasonable person in a like situation, seeing and knowing the same facts, would be justified in believing himself in like danger, and if that individual so confronted acts in self-defense upon these appearances and from that fear and actual beliefs, the person's right of self-defense is the same whether the danger is real or merely apparent.

Texas provides another useful example in its jury instructions:

Texas

§3:1730 Limitations on Self-Defense a. Apparent Danger Instruction
Because the reasonableness of the actor's belief that force or deadly force was immediately necessary is judged from the standpoint of an ordinary person in the same circumstances as the actor, a person has a right to defend from apparent danger to the same extent as he would had the danger been real; provided he acted upon a reasonable apprehension of danger as it appeared to him at the time.

Presumptions of Reasonableness

You may recall that all defendants are presumed innocent until proven guilty. In the same way, a presumption of reasonableness establishes that your actions were reasonable until proven unreasonable.

At least 23 states provide you with a "presumption of reasonableness" in some scenarios—usually those happening in the context of highly-defensible property, which states variously define for various purposes as including a home (pretty much universally), sometimes a place of business, and sometimes occupied vehicle.

Importantly, such presumptions of reasonableness are usually highly conditional, meaning if you fail to check any of the required boxes, you don't qualify for this presumption. Typical conditions include that the person you used force against did, or was attempting to, forcibly and unlawfully enter the highly-defensible property. If that condition is not met, the legal presumption is not triggered.

If the conditions are met in these states, however, the judge instructs the jury on both your presumed innocence and presumed reasonableness. Now the jury considers you an innocent and reasonable person, until proven otherwise. This will reinforce to the jury that the prosecution's threshold is a high one, indeed. It also reminds prosecutors just how hard it will be to undermine you on this principle.

Wrap-Up

The fifth fundamental element of the law of self-defense is Reasonableness, which has both objective and subjective components.

Objectively, the law requires that your actions be the same as a reasonable and prudent person, in the same or similar circumstances, who possesses the same physical characteristics, specialized knowledge, and (some) mental characteristics as you did at the time you used defensive force.

You must have known any specialized knowledge that you wish to use at trial to justify reasonableness at the time of the encounter, not later. There are limited exceptions to this condition, in the context of your attacker's reputation for or history of violence.

Typical human emotion can be applied to the reasonable and prudent person. Aberrant mental states, such as psychiatric conditions and drunkenness, are not. The one exception is Battered Spouse Syndrome.

Subjectively, the law requires that you had a genuine, good faith belief that your actions were reasonable and necessary self-defense, on each of the elements.

Neither objective or subjective reasonableness alone is sufficient to satisfy the requirements of this element of Reasonableness—you must have both.

Reasonable mistakes do not doom your claim of self-defense. If you reasonably think your attacker's fake gun was real, you are allowed to treat it as if it were real. We are not required to make perfect decisions in self-defense, we are merely required to make reasonable decisions in self-defense.

Nearly half the states have "presumptions of reasonableness" in the context of your home, place of business, or occupied vehicle, but these are triggered only if the required, and often complex, conditions are met.

Chapter 7

A Legally Sound Defense Strategy

And here we are, the chapter where we bring it all together. Each of the previous chapters was a building block for what we seek to accomplish in this one: crafting a legally sound self-defense strategy.

Here we discuss defensive tactics and strategies that win the physical fight (our top priority) *and* the legal fight.

Out in the real world, of course, there are a nearly infinite number of self-defense strategies people recommend. Some are better than others. If you are considering adopting any, I urge you to evaluate them in the context of the five elements of the law of self-defense, as we've covered them in this book. Does a given strategy weaken or strengthen your lawyer's arguments on any of the 5 elements? If it weakens an argument, is increasing your legal vulnerability counter-balanced by a survival benefit?

It should go without saying that something that increases your likelihood of jail and doesn't help your survival is a bad idea.

For example: If you inscribe "Thug Killer" on your pistol's slide, will that turn a clean self-defense shoot into a murder conviction? Maybe not. But could it turn a marginal self-defense shoot into manslaughter? Quite possibly. And even if the increased legal risk is only minimal, is it offset by a higher likelihood of survival? I doubt it—that inscription doesn't help your gun run better or improve your aim. It is, in my opinion, a very poor tradeoff.

Avoidance

The first thing I recommend you incorporate into your self-defense strategy is avoidance. I use this term tactically, not legally. Avoidance from a tactical perspective prevents involvement or engagement entirely, perhaps long before the encounter could ever happen. In large part, this involves simply not being where the fight happens.

From my perspective, avoidance is the highest form of fighting. If successful, it reduces both your physical and legal risk to zero. Every option after avoidance has some greater-than-zero risk of death, a lifetime in jail, and financial ruin. As the famed military strategist Sun Tzu put it:

> "The supreme art of war is to subdue the enemy without fighting."

In our context, you are "subduing the enemy" when you deny your attacker the opportunity to attack you in the first place.

To quote the excellent Rory Miller from his book *Facing Violence*:

> "It is better to avoid than to run, better to run than to de-escalate, better to de-escalate than to fight, better to fight than to die."[3]

The key to avoidance is situational awareness. If you're not aware of your environment, well, you're just prey waiting to be taken.

That said, I don't mean situational awareness in a superficial "snapshot of your immediate surroundings" kind of way. That kind of awareness is necessary to avoidance but it is not by itself sufficient. What I'm suggesting as an alternative to a snapshot type of awareness is more of a forecasting type of awareness.

---

[3] Incidentally, I personally read everything that Rory Miller writes, and highly recommend you check his work out as well.

The environment around you is constantly changing, and you are constantly transitioning through new environments—entering and exiting vehicles, stores, and so forth.

These factors create a significant fluidity to your surroundings, and therefore your awareness needs to be similarly fluid. You need to be aware not just of your current situation but also of the coming situation. You need to, in a way, predict the future. But isn't that impossible?

Well, yes and no. While you can't know exactly what is going to happen, it is possible to develop a keen sense of what will likely happen, or if something seems to be not quite right. I refer to this as "maturity of foresight."

All experienced drivers do this automatically. We're not just aware of the roadway immediately in front of our bumper.

Our eyes scan further ahead. We see the brake lights on the car a quarter-mile down the road, so we lift our foot off the gas, laying it weightlessly above the brake. We don't yet know if we'll need to slow or stop, but we know we might need to. Novice drivers have higher rates of accidents in part because they have yet to develop this ability.

Any of us who are parents have seen our younger kids struggle with similar challenges in foresight. They take a glass full of bright red juice and place it on a table so that 49% of the glass is over the edge. This kind of thing leaves a parent flabbergasted.

As adults, we know what's going to happen—a permanent red stain on our carpet. We apply our maturity of foresight routinely, perhaps 95% of the time. Children, however, lack this maturity of foresight. They're genuinely surprised when the totally foreseeable spill happens.

As people who carry arms, we have contemplated the possibility of taking a human life in necessary self-defense, and are prepared to do so. But taking life is the last option, so we must apply that maturity of foresight to our surroundings to minimize the risk of finding ourselves at that gravest extreme.

And we need to apply that maturity of foresight always, 100% of the time, zero downtime.

I don't know that the Bible is always the go-to source for self-defense strategies, legal or otherwise, but there's a quote from *1 Corinthians* that I find very fitting in this context:

> "When I was a child, I spoke as a child, I understood as a child, I thought as a child; but

when I became a man, I put away childish things."

1 Corinthians 13:11, NKJV

When I became a man—and I think of it as an armed man—I put away childish things . . . as must we all, if we intend to replace those "childish things" with a concealed firearm.

Part of this requires learning how to be aware of your environment in a more forward-looking manner than you might be used to. You need to learn how to recognize bad terrain—like ambush zones—before you suddenly find yourself in the midst of that terrain.

In the wild, predators know prey must come to watering holes regularly. All life needs water, so the predators set up to ambush the prey while there.

Watering holes also exist in modern human societies. A great example is the gas station. Cars need to drink too, after all. While you're fueling up, you're distracted. You have your wallet or purse out, you've brought a multi-thousand dollar automobile with you, complete with the keys, and there are gas pumps and other cars that obscure your view of the immediate environment.

What more could a predator ask for? Many predators don't—that's plenty, and that's when they attack their prey.

Of course, anyone with a car must, from time to time, go to a gas station. It's unavoidable. While you're there, however, be aware that you're at a watering hole. You have enough distractions just gassing up; don't add more by checking your smartphone for emails. Keep your eyes up and look around. Don't allow yourself to be surprised.

Also, not all gas stations are equal. I travel many times a year to teach my Law of Self Defense classes. The rental car I get when I arrive needs to be refueled before I return it to the airport, so I'm obliged to go to a watering hole.

That does not mean, though, that I need to go to the gas station/watering hole that looks sketchy as heck when I pull up. As Gavin de Becker advises in his excellent *The Gift of Fear*, if those alarm bells are going off in your head, don't simply ignore them. Drive on by, and keep going to the next gas station. Or the one after that, if doing so seems prudent.

Where else are there environmental dangers? John Farnham's oft-repeated warning "the three don'ts" nicely summarizes how to avoid the vast majority of bad situations:

> Don't do stupid things.
> Don't go to stupid places.
> Don't hang out with stupid people.

If you can abide by those three rules, I expect you'd avoid 99% of the trouble that life can throw at you.

That said, this is really more an aspiration than a mandate. After all, where does much of the joy in life come from?

So I'm not telling you to never do any of these three things. But if you are doing one of them, be aware that you are, in fact, in a higher-risk environment than would otherwise be the case.

Conduct yourself accordingly.

Escape/Retreat

Sometimes circumstances require a fight. As we've already discussed, though, fighting is what you do when there is no better option. If safely possible, cut your physical and legal vulnerability by escaping from an engagement.

In a nutshell, if it is safely possible to retreat, for Pete's sake, retreat.

Retreat provides tactical advantages, even above and beyond escape. If you end up having to fight despite your efforts to retreat, those efforts still increase your distance from the attacker. And greater distance is greater reaction time. That's a tremendous tactical advantage.

Remember the Tueller Drill. If you'd have 1.5 seconds to react to a threat 21 feet away, each additional foot of distance gives you even more time to react. Time gives us options, which gives us freedom of action, which is always a good thing.

Retreating also minimizes your legal vulnerability. Remember, the jury doesn't know what happened in any absolute sense. They can come to a verdict based only on what the evidence suggests happened.

A prosecutor would love to spin the evidence into a story where you were the aggressor. But if surveillance video shows you backing up, hands at chest level, palms out, the prosecutor's job just got much harder.

Now let's imagine, horror of horrors, that you momentarily lost your mind and really were the aggressor—what have you done by withdrawing from the confrontation and communicating your withdrawal?

That's right. You've regained your innocence.

That's the benefit of retreat from the standpoint of Innocence. What about the Imminence? If you're successfully retreating from an armed aggressor, they now have to pursue you to continue the fight.

If they pursue you while you're yelling at them to stay away, their pursuit is demonstrably jeopardy, the "J" of the AOJ Triad. Assuming ability ("A") and opportunity ("O") are also present, the fight is now clearly imminent.

The False Security of Being Armed

Many people believe that a gun strapped to their hip means they don't have to take guff from anybody. If you're one of those people, correct that perception now. The truth could not be more the opposite.

Now that you're carrying a gun, you've got to take guff from *everybody*.

Except the guy trying to kill, maim, rape, or kidnap you, or who is trying to break into your home. That guy you can defend yourself against with the gun.

Everyone else? Not so much.

Why do I emphasize this point? Because clients get into trouble by misjudging this legal reality.

If a guy flips the bird at you after he cuts you off in traffic, even the slightest response from you can be spun against you. A good prosecutor will say you wanted an excuse to use your gun.

And if you lose the legal battle, using your gun will be an aggravating factor of both your criminal charge and your sentence. Fumbling avoidance can carry far scarier legal consequences when armed.

That's not an argument for you to not carry concealed—I carry concealed myself, and have my entire adult life. I'm all in favor of law-abiding, mentally sound American citizens carrying deadly weapons for defense. It's only a caution to do so in an informed manner.

De-Escalation

Well, this isn't good. You've failed to avoid, and you've failed to escape. Or perhaps there was no chance to begin with to do either. Now what?

Time to de-escalate the confrontation. De-escalation is pretty much the last ramp off the highway that will otherwise lead to a hands-on (or guns-out) fight.

There are innumerable tactical approaches to de-escalation. Many require a sophisticated understanding of predators and how they differ (e.g., resource predators versus process predators). I again recommend Rory Miller's excellent work for guidance on such issues.

Verbal Defense

A great de-escalation technique is one we all possess, and is surprisingly effective. I'm talking about verbal defense, or what some call command voice.

Get loud.

Verbally engage your attacker, loudly and confidently. Doing so can yield tremendous tactical and legal benefits.

Remember when I said predators prefer easy prey? When you yell, you look harder. Indeed, if you're loud enough you begin to look like a genuine pain in the behind. If predators had a work ethic, they wouldn't be thugs —yelling alone may well be enough to encourage your predator to look for easier prey elsewhere.

Yelling also generates evidence. What do we all do, instinctively, if we hear someone shouting nearby? We turn and look. Well, when you get loud, other people turn and look — we call those people witnesses.

Good guys acting in self-defense should want unbiased witnesses, and plenty of them. Good guy cases of self-defense are far more likely to suffer from too little evidence in a case, leaving their claim of self-defense looking fabricated or speculative, than they are from too much evidence.

Guess what else might happen when you start attracting people's attention? Somebody might come to help you. You could even encourage this by shouting, "Help!"

Perhaps the greatest legal value of command voice is that it can effectively strip the ambiguity out of an unclear encounter.

Say a woman is walking alone at night through a parking garage. The garage is empty except for her, a handful of cars ... and some unfamiliar guy walking 30 feet behind her.

There's something about that guy that's genuinely scaring her. Is he following her? Or is his car just by happenstance parked near hers? Why is she so scared? And I mean really scared, approaching almost paralyzing physiological fear. Her mental alarm bells are going crazy.

Yet, the man hasn't yet done anything explicitly threatening. She can't simply turn around and shoot him!

The good news is she does have a gun and knows how to use it. If the man does become a clear and imminent deadly force threat, she is prepared to defend herself. If he pulls out a knife and approaches her, she'll shoot him without hesitation.

But that's the question, isn't it? Is he a clear threat? He hasn't pulled out a knife. Yet. It's terrifying. What can she do?

She can use verbal commands to strip away the ambiguity. Force the man to either stop what he's doing that's frightening her, or to act consistently with being a threat and thereby expose his intent to harm.

What might such a verbal defense look like—or, more appropriately, sound like? She could spin around to face the man (before he gets too close), hold her palm out in the universal signal for "STOP!" and shout, "GET AWAY FROM ME!!!!"

If that man is a good guy who just happens to be walking in the same direction for perfectly harmless reasons, how will he respond to that kind of challenge? He'll probably get as far from her as possible, the crazy lunatic. And what's the worst that she's done? She yelled at a stranger. Try getting charged with a crime for *that*.

If he doesn't make himself scarce, if he continues to close despite repeated demands that he stay back, is he a predator intent on causing harm? Yep. Does she now have a reasonable and evidence-based basis to infer that he is an imminent threat? Absolutely.

See what she's done here? She used verbal defense to strip the ambiguity out of the scenario. Either the guy stops doing what was frightening her and goes away, or he continues to engage in conduct that is now, in the context of the verbal challenge, clearly threatening.

Defensive Display

What if yelling at an attacker doesn't work? Remember, avoidance and escape are already off the table. Either they failed, or there was no opportunity to try them.

The next step in our legally sound self-defense strategy is defensive display of the firearm. We talked about defensive display in some detail already in the chapter on the element of Imminence, and I'm not going to repeat all that here. I'll just add a few more thoughts.

First, while I do not encourage premature defensive display, when it does become tactically and legally appropriate to draw your gun, you won't have time to hesitate. The scenario goes "Don't display ... don't display ... don't display ... DISPLAY NOW!!!!!"

Swift defensive display, when appropriate, has both tactical and legal benefits. If you practice your draw so it's under a second, you can delay the moment you have to draw for real—and that's more time for you to try to avoid, escape, and de-escalate verbally.

On the other hand, lack of necessary skill may drive a panicked response. You may show too much force, too early, increasing your legal vulnerability.

Diversified Toolbox

We talked in Chapter 4 on Proportionality about how important it is to carry a non-deadly weapon. Remember, you are five times more likely to be the victim of a non-deadly force attack than a deadly force attack.

I've carried a concealed firearm my entire adult life. It's the single best tool I have to defend my family and myself from deadly force—to ensure that we're hard to kill. When my gun is on my person, though, so is my pepper spray.[4] Anyone who prepares only for a deadly force threat sets himself or herself up for going disproportional, and unlawfully so, if faced with a real, serious, non-deadly threat.

Don't paint yourself into that corner.

Cognitive Conditioning

How do you make decisions under the stress of a life-and-death encounter? The same way the police and military do it. Know the rules of the game, and train to operate within those rules as automatically, and with as much subconscious competence, as possible.

You may be thinking, *Holy cow, I just read this whole book—and it's a fire hose of information. And I still need to find my state's laws online. How could I possibly make that much knowledge "automatic"?*

If you drive a car, you've already done this on a far greater scale. For many people learning to drive it's

---

[4] OC is my preferred non-deadly force defensive weapon, given the laws and options where I live.

common to feel like there's an overwhelming amount of information to remember and process.

OK, steering wheel, gas, brakes—that's not so bad. Wait, there's a clutch and a gear lever. But wait, there are also mirrors—three of them! A turn signal indicator. Where's the parking brake? Oops, I'm going too fast, now I'm braking too slow. Am I in my lane? How do I tell?? ...OK that other car's getting kind of close . . .

It can be harrowing for a student driver (and arguably even worse for the parent trying to teach them!).

But, for most of us, it wasn't long before we were driving, adjusting the radio, drinking a latte, talking on our cell phones, smoking a cigarette, putting on makeup, and breaking up an argument between the kids in the back seat.

All at the same time!

Well, hopefully not all at the same time, but you get the point. So much of the driving skill had become automatic that we had freed our mental bandwidth for other tasks.

In the context of a self-defense encounter, you do not want to be spending a lot of your mental bandwidth trying to remember the laws in your state. You want to be able to make critical, perhaps life-and-death tactical decisions, with a generous amount of cognitive bandwidth still available—not just because you'll make the best decisions that way, but also because you'll need the bandwidth for situational awareness.

But how do you accomplish this under the stress of a life-and-death attack? There are mental "tricks" you can "program" into your head to make quicker, better decisions with fewer mental resources. While it seems there is an infinite variety of ways a bad guy can threaten you or your family, as a practical matter you can place these scenarios into generalized buckets, with each bucket having a limited menu of responses.

For example, some scenarios might go into the "will always retreat" bucket. Others might go into the "only non-deadly defensive force" bucket. A very few scenarios might go into the "deadly force now!" bucket. You'll need to use your knowledge of self-defense law and your own ethical/moral standards to define your own personalized buckets. Once your buckets have been defined, you don't have to evaluate every real-life scenario from first principles, but can start reacting to the threat several steps down the decision path.

Using this strategy can offset the inherent tactical advantage attackers are used to enjoying because of their ability to choose the time, place, and manner of attack. A defender who responds decisively and much more quickly than the typical victim can often seize the action-reaction high ground to good tactical effect.

I'm not encouraging you to be robotically reflexive: "If I see A, then I'll instantly do B." Rather, I'm suggesting you reduce the number of decisions you'll need to make while under the influence of physiological fear and the reduced mental bandwidth that goes with it. Automate the decisions that can be responsibly automated, so you can focus on the ones that require genuine real-time cognitive effort.

Now that you've made what decisions you could in advance, stay flexible. Allow for a different course of action, depending on the developing facts you find yourself facing.

Also, maintain your skills. If all you do is read this book once, then shelve it, and don't make any effort to keep the information fresh in your mind, then you won't be able to make effective use of this critical knowledge under stress when you most need it.

Any of you who shoot competitively know what I'm talking about. You may be at the very top of your game, but if you take a couple of months away from handling that firearm, those skills degrade rapidly. After two months without practice, if you try to shoot a match, you'll do poorly compared to your skill level when you had been practicing.

So don't just read this book and put it away. Leave it out in an accessible place, where you'll see it on a regular basis. Occasionally pick it up, open to a random page, and read for a few minutes. A couple of pages every day would be awesome. (Some people suggest that the bathroom is a good place for this, but I leave that to your discretion.)

When you hear about a self-defense event in the news, use what you've learned in the book and the materials at lawofselfdefense.com/resources to conduct your own legal analysis based on your state. Where were the person's five elements of self-defense strong? Where were they weak? How might they have been strengthened? What could they have done to mitigate their legal vulnerability and still win the physical fight?

I do just this kind of analysis on my *After Action Analysis* show, which you can access at that our website— http://lawofselfdefense.com.

In short, had you been in their place, what would you have done to ensure the strongest possible compelling narrative of lawful self-defense, consistent with winning the physical fight?

This is similar to how airplane pilots train for in-flight emergencies. They run through simulations of those scenarios, automate the responses that can be reasonably automated, and free up bandwidth to evaluate the details that are unique to each scenario.

Pilots also have highly sophisticated computer-driven simulators. Increasingly, so do defensive instructors. At Law of Self Defense we have long incorporated a self-defense simulator into our in-person classes, so that students who complete the classroom experience can apply their just-acquired knowledge in a simulated (yet remarkably stressful) self-defense situation.

Even if you don't have access to those kinds of resources, though, you can do much the same by yourself, in your head, by applying what you've learned in this book to use-of-force events in the news, or as covered in our own weekly *After Action Analysis* shows.

The best part? You can do that at absolutely no cost. It's the self-defense law equivalent of dry firing, and just as useful.

Wrap-Up

The key to minimizing your legal liability to indictment, prosecution, conviction, or lawsuit is to understand how your use-of-force will be judged.

Understand the "rules of the game," the five elements of the law of self-defense. Know what conduct and scenarios generate evidence that makes your compelling narrative of lawful self-defense stronger, or weaker.

Then, adopt strategies and tactics that strengthen your narrative of innocence, and avoid those that weaken it, to make the prosecutor's job a great deal harder.

To do so, avoid problems before they arise, retreat whenever safely possible, de-escalate by using command voice and other strategies, have a diversified toolbox to work with, and condition yourself cognitively to be ready when the fight comes to you.

Learn More

And ... that's it. You've done it. You've finished understanding the law of self-defense in its entirety. Congratulations.

Well, not really, of course. You now have a solid foundation of how the laws work generally. But your state's laws can vary from the general rule as we have commonly discussed in this book. I recommend your next step to be to obtain a high level of understanding about your state's laws by going to lawofselfdefense.com/resources. This book will help you understand the laws provided to you on that page so you are best prepared for the unexpected.

But there is still much more you can learn. To help with this, Law of Self Defense offers opportunities for a more in-depth education on use-of-force law in several forms.

Membership (FREE!)

Easiest of all, sign up for our Law of Self Defense membership program to stay up-to-date on self-defense law, and particularly how it is applied to real people in real use-of-force cases.

Our lowest level of membership is absolutely free, so there's really no reason not to sign up.

There are also higher levels of membership, with higher levels of benefits, but I urge you to sign up for at least our free level, and learn about the other levels if you like, here:

lawofselfdefense.com/join

State-Specific Classes

Our state-specific classes (presented by me) cover your state's nuanced laws. Self-paced and convenient, these lectures use YOUR state's statutes, case law and jury instructions then break them down from legalese into plain English to help you devise an actionable self-defense plan. Learn when and where you prefer and progress as quickly or slowly as you like. Available in both streaming and DVD format, you can get your state's class here:

> **lawofselfdefense.com/state**

CONSULT Program

Knowing what to do before the attack goes an enormous way to being safe from prosecution. But you never know for sure. That's why I developed the LOSD CONSULT Program. Sign up below and be guaranteed should you face charges I will drop everything I'm doing to consult on your case, for a fraction of the normal price:

> **lawofselfdefense.com/consult**

Instructor Program

If you are a self-defense instructor and wish you could cover use-of-force law with much greater detail and certainty, our Instructor Program is perfect for your needs. This is the most in-depth instruction available from any source — including law school — on use-of-force law.

You can find more information on the Instructor Program here:

lawofselfdefense.com/instructor-program

Stay safe, and remember, you carry a gun so you're hard to kill. Know the law so you're hard to convict.

-Andrew

About The Author

Andrew F. Branca, Esq. is currently in his third decade of practicing law, and is an internationally-recognized expert on the law of self-defense of the United States. Andrew is an active legal consultant on use-of-force cases involving serious felony charges on a nationwide basis.

As a certified Continuing Legal Education instructor in self-defense law in more than 30 states, Andrew also teaches criminal defense attorneys, prosecutors, and judges how to argue for, defend against, and rule on self-defense cases.

Andrew has been a Guest Lecturer at the Federal Bureau of Investigation's National Academy, is a graduate of the Force Science Institute, has been a co-host on the Outdoor Channel's TV show "The Best Defense",

As a subject-matter expert on use-of-force law, Andrew has contributed to National Review, and is cited as an expert on self-defense law by the Wall Street Journal, the Chicago Tribune, the Washington Post, as well as nationally syndicated print and broadcast media.

Andrew is also an NRA Life-Benefactor Member, and an NRA Certified Instructor, and a Life Member of the Second Amendment Foundation, amongst othe civil rights organizations.

In addition to being a lawyer, Andrew has also been a life-long competitive handgun shooter, is an IDPA Charter/Life member (IDPA #13), and has competed at the Master-class level in multiple IDPA divisions on a national level. .

For more information on Andrew and Law of Self Defense, please visit www.lawofselfdefense.com.